Facilitator's Guide

WHAT EVERY PRINCIPAL SHOULD KNOW ABOUT

LEADERSHIP

JEFFREY GLANZ

CORWIN PRESS
A SAGE Publications Company
Thousand Oaks, California

For information:

Corwin Press
A Sage Publications Company
2455 Teller Road
Thousand Oaks, California 91320
E-mail: order@corwinpress.com

Sage Publications Ltd.
1 Oliver's Yard
55 City Road
London EC1Y 1SP
United Kingdom

Sage Publications India Pvt. Ltd.
B-42, Panchsheel Enclave
Post Box 4109
New Delhi 110 017 India

ISBN 1-4129-4136-9

06 07 08 09 10 11 9 8 7 6 5 4 3 2 1

Acquisitions Editor:	Elizabeth Brenkus
Editorial Assistant:	Desirée Enayati
Project Editor:	Tracy Alpern
Copy Editor:	Annette Pagliaro
Proofreader:	Libby Larson
Typesetter:	C&M Digitals (P) Ltd.
Cover Designer:	Rose Storey

Contents

About the Author   v

Introduction   vi

    Organization of the Facilitator's Guide   vi

    How to Use the Guide   vii

    Overview of the Principalship: Discussion Questions   viii

    K-W-L Activity   xi

    Interview Questions   xii

Part I—Book One: *What Every Principal Should Know About Instructional Leadership*   1

    Overview of Instructional Leadership   1

    Best Practices in Teaching   2

    Best Practices in Curriculum   4

    Best Practices in Supervision and Professional Development   6

    Best Practices in Promoting Student Achievement   8

    Culminating Activity   10

    Instructional Leadership Reproducibles   12

Part II—Book Two: *What Every Principal Should Know About Cultural Leadership*   26

    Overview of Cultural Leadership   26

    Best Practices in Sustaining Positive Organizational
       Climate and Culture   27

    Best Practices in Visionary Leadership   28

    Best Practices in Promoting Cultural Diversity Leadership   29

    Best Practices in Fostering Organization
       Self-Renewal Leadership   30

    Culminating Activity   32

    Cultural Leadership Reproducibles   33

Part III—Book Three: *What Every Principal Should Know About Ethical and Spiritual Leadership*   47

    Overview of Ethical and Spiritual Leadership   47

    Best Practices in Leading Ethically, With Moral
       Purpose, and With an Awareness of the Spiritual   48

    Best Practices for Leading With Soul and Conviction   49

    Best Practices for Resolving Ethical Dilemmas   51

    Culminating Activity   52

    Ethical and Spiritual Leadership Reproducibles   53

Part IV—Book Four: *What Every Principal Should Know About School-Community Leadership* 68

    Overview of School-Community Leadership 68

    Best Practices in Reaching Out to Parents 69

    Best Practices in Building Community Alliances 70

    Best Practices to Close the Black-White Achievement Gap 72

    Culminating Activity 73

    School-Community Leadership Reproducibles 74

Part V—Book Five: *What Every Principal Should Know About Collaborative Leadership* 87

    Overview of Collaborative Leadership 87

    Best Practices in Team Building 88

    Best Practices in Action Research 89

    Best Practices in Shared Decision Making 90

    Culminating Activity 92

    Collaborative Leadership Reproducibles 93

Part VI—Book Six: *What Every Principal Should Know About Operational Leadership* 111

    Overview of Operational Leadership 111

    Best Practices in Getting Organized 111

    Best Practices in Managing Facilities 112

    Best Practice in School Finance and Handling the Budget 113

    Best Practices in Human Resources Management 114

    Best Practices in Communicating Effectively 116

    Best Practices in Personal Management 117

    Culminating Activity 118

    Operational Leadership Reproducibles 120

Part VII—Book Seven: *What Every Principal Should Know About Strategic Leadership* 146

    Overview of Strategic Leadership 146

    Best Practices in Planning Strategically 147

    Best Practices in Data-Driven Decision Making 148

    Best Practices in Transformational Leadership 149

    Culminating Activity 150

    Strategic Leadership Reproducibles 152

Sample Workshop Agendas 162

    Half-Day Workshop Agendas 162

    One-Day Workshop Agendas 167

Workshop Evaluation Form 174

References 175

About the Author

 **Jeffrey Glanz, EdD**, currently serves as Dean of Graduate Programs and Chair of the Department of Education at Wagner College in Staten Island, New York. He also coordinates the educational leadership program that leads to New York State certification as a principal and assistant principal. Prior to arriving at Wagner, he served as executive assistant to the president of Kean University in Union, New Jersey. Dr. Glanz held faculty status as a tenured professor in the Department of Instruction and Educational Leadership at Kean University's College of Education. He was named Graduate Teacher of the Year in 1999 by the Student Graduate Association and was also that year's recipient of the Presidential Award for Outstanding Scholarship. He served as an administrator and teacher in the New York City public schools for 20 years. Dr. Glanz has authored, coauthored, and coedited 20 books and has many peer-reviewed article publications. With Corwin Press he coauthored the bestselling *Supervision That Improves Teaching* (2nd ed.), *Supervision in Practice: Three Steps to Improve Teaching and Learning*, authored *The Assistant Principal's Handbook* and *Teaching 101: Strategies for the Beginning Teacher*, and more recently coauthored *Building Effective Learning Communities: Strategies for Leadership, Learning, & Collaboration*. Most recently, Dr. Glanz has authored *What Every Principal Should Know About Leadership: The 7-Book Collection:*

What Every Principal Should Know About Instructional Leadership

What Every Principal Should Know About Cultural Leadership

What Every Principal Should Know About Ethical and Spiritual Leadership

What Every Principal Should Know About School-Community Leadership

What Every Principal Should Know About Collaborative Leadership

What Every Principal Should Know About Operational Leadership

What Every Principal Should Know About Strategic Leadership

Dr. Glanz offers his services as consultant and workshop presenter.

Consult his Web site for additional information: http://www.wagner.edu/faculty/jglanz/.

Introduction

Organization of the Facilitator's Guide

This Facilitator's Guide is a companion for *What Every Principal Should Know About Leadership: The 7-Book Collection* by Jeffrey Glanz. It is designed to accompany the study of each book in the series and provide assistance to group facilitators, such as school and district leaders, professional development coordinators, consultants, mentors, and professors. It can also be used by students in leadership courses leading to certification for the principalship as a guide to teach each other various concepts or reinforce certain principles. A professor I know uses this creative strategy to reinforce student learning. In other words, he feels that if students are able to "teach" something to someone else, they will, in the process, gain greater facility with the material. Along a similar line of thinking, the guide can serve to stimulate ideas for student presentations.

The guide is divided into seven parts, each representing one book in the series. After a brief overview of the type of leadership addressed in the book, "Best Practices" are highlighted. For each "Best Practice" discussed, an overview is presented along with relevant discussion questions and at least one "Engagement Activity." This Facilitator's Guide should obviously be used in conjunction with each book, as the guide will refer the user to relevant pages in the text. Along with the material in this guide, I have provided key handouts that can be copied (labeled as Reproducibles), if needed, and used to develop one's own PowerPoint presentations. A few PowerPoint presentations (i.e., one on action research, one on leadership styles, one on the assistant principalship, and one of all seven forms of principal leadership) can be downloaded from the author's Web site: http://www.wagner.edu/faculty/jglanz/ppoint. Users of this guide are free to download the PowerPoint files and use them as presented or make revisions as necessary. As long as proper credit is given for the source of the PowerPoints and handouts (Reproducibles), they may be used without expressed advance permission. Sample half-day, full-day, and two-day workshop agendas are included.

Corwin Press also offers a free 16-page resource titled *Tips for Facilitators,* which provides the facilitator with practical strategies and tips for guiding a successful meeting. The information in this resource describes different professional development opportunities, the principles of effective professional development, some characteristics of an effective facilitator, the responsibilities of the facilitator, and practical tips and strategies to make meetings more successful. *Tips for Facilitators* is available for free download from the Corwin Press Web site (www.corwinpress .com, click on "Extras").

How to Use the Guide

If you have skipped the introductory section on page vi, please read it as it may contain an idea or two you've not thought about and may lead you to some handy references or materials to assist in presenting information from the various books in the series.

Become familiar with the content of the volume in the series in which you are presenting. Each book in the series is approximately 100 pages or so with an easy-to-read layout to facilitate quick reading. Peruse the contents of the Facilitator's Guide to study various options or alternative ways of presenting information as well as the various materials offered. Also, go to the Web site http://www.wagner.edu/faculty/jglanz/ppoint to peruse the PowerPoints. With such an overview, you'll be able to select appropriate parts of the guide for your special needs. Obviously, the guide is not meant to be read from cover to cover but to be used as a resource of ideas and materials to choose from depending on your purpose and needs. Various options are provided in the section of this guide titled "Sample Workshop Agendas."

Use the general *discussion questions* in the next section to perhaps begin to stimulate thinking among participants as a Starter Activity. Often, attendees of workshops seem to expect, if not enjoy, some downtime by sitting back and "listening." Engaging them in small group discussions (you may first want them to pair-and-share), followed by whole group brainstorming may set a positive and interactive tone for the remainder of your time with them. Besides, such early engagement will enhance learning because, as you very well know, we learn best by constructing meaning on our own.

Assess the knowledge and skills that you currently possess and that you wish or need to learn in order to become an effective principal by doing the *K-W-L Activity* as another starter activity. Such an activity will prompt deep thinking about the principalship and serve to identify areas that require investigation. Articulating precise areas of knowledge needed for serving as principal, specialized skills of performance, and unique qualities or dispositions will set the tone for your study of the principalship. Individuals who serve as effective principals possess unique characteristics and display special behaviors that set them apart from other education professionals in the school building. Not everyone who serves as an assistant principal, for instance, can serve effectively as principal. Explore these unique and necessary areas of knowledge, skills, and dispositions.

Use the *Interview Questions* as yet another starter activity to motivate participants and encourage critical and creative thinking about the principalship. Note that the list of questions is not meant to be exhaustive, but, rather, should be used to prompt thinking. Also, these are real questions that have been posed at interviews. Some questions are "out of the box," as you will see. Pair-and-share, form small groups, then large ones, or perhaps use the fishbowl technique. Role-playing with volunteers should be encouraged. If, after this exercise, participants feel that they need additional information (which many will), refer them to various books in the Leadership Series, as appropriate.

I recommend that facilitators download a copy of *Tips for Facilitators* and review the characteristics and responsibilities of facilitators and professional development strategies for different types of work groups and settings.

Overview of the Principalship: Discussion Questions

The following discussion questions are appropriate for individuals studying to become a principal.

Reproducible 1:
Discussion Questions for Future Principals

1. Describe why you want to become a principal.

2. What in your background and experiences might be significant in terms of your desire to become a principal?

3. Which individuals have influenced or inspired you to become a principal?

4. Can you recall and describe a principal or two who does not serve as a role model? What did they do or not do to categorize themselves as ineffective? Keep responses anonymous.

5. What are the three areas or topics you hope will be covered in [this session] or [in your principal preparation program]?

6. Should a principal be expected to have expertise in each of these areas: instructional, cultural, ethical/spiritual, school-community, collaborative, operational, and strategic? Explain why or why not.

7. What is your philosophy of leadership as a future principal?

8. Did your role as assistant principal prepare you for the principalship? Explain. If you weren't an assistant principal, then what about the position you currently hold?

9. What do you expect your three greatest challenges will be in the first year or two as principal?

10. Do you aspire to a position beyond the principalship?

The following discussion questions are appropriate for individuals who have just completed or are in the process of completing their first year or two as principal.

Reproducible 2:
Discussion Questions for Beginning Principals

1. Describe your experiences as a fairly new principal. What have been your greatest challenges? Successes?

2. Recall how you responded when asked why you wanted to become a principal. Are the reasons similar now, given your initial experiences as principal?

3. What advice would you give a brand new principal in your district/region?

4. Which individuals have supported you the most during your first year or two?

5. How and what do you delegate to others?

6. What responsibilities have you decided to handle personally?

7. How would you rate your performance as principal thus far?

8. What are the three areas or topics you need to know more about so that you can serve with even more success as principal?

9. Should a principal be expected to have expertise in each of these areas: instructional, cultural, ethical/spiritual, school-community, collaborative, operational, and strategic? Explain why or why not.

10. What is your philosophy of leadership as a new principal?

11. Did your role as assistant principal prepare you for the principalship? Explain. If you weren't an assistant principal, then what about the position you held prior to the principalship?

The following discussion questions are appropriate for individuals who have been serving as principals for three or more years.

Reproducible 3:
Discussion Questions for Experienced Principals

1. Describe your experiences as an experienced principal. What have been your greatest challenges? Successes?

2. Recall how you responded when asked many years ago why you wanted to become a principal. Are the reasons similar now, given your experiences as principal?

3. What advice would you give a brand new principal in your district/region?

4. Which individuals have supported you the most during your tenure as principal?

5. How and what do you delegate to others?

6. What responsibilities have you decided to handle personally?

7. How would you rate your performance as principal thus far?

8. What are the three areas or topics you need to know more about so that you can serve with even more success as principal?

9. Should a principal be expected to have expertise in each of these areas: instructional, cultural, ethical/spiritual, school-community, collaborative, operational, and strategic? Explain why or why not.

10. What is your philosophy of leadership as a principal?

11. Did your role as assistant principal prepare you for the principalship? Explain. If you weren't an assistant principal, then what about the position you held prior to the principalship?

K-W-L Activity

Employing the K-W-L strategy developed by Donna Sederburg Ogle (1986) is a most effective strategy that models active thinking needed before, during, and after learning. The letters **K**, **W**, and **L** stand for three activities participants engage in when learning: recalling what they KNOW, determining what they WANT to learn, and identifying what they have LEARNED (see Figure 1).

WHAT I KNOW	WHAT I WANT TO LEARN	WHAT I LEARNED

Figure 1   K-W-L Strategy Sheet

Encourage participants to write out what they know about serving as principal, what questions they want answered, and what they have learned after a particular session or unit of instruction. Participants can individually or in small groups record their responses and then share their information with the whole group.

Interview Questions

Practice these 30 interview questions in small groups (divide groups and assign certain questions; e.g., five groups with six questions each):

1. What skills do you bring to a task?

2. Describe your ideal school.

3. What was the last novel you read?

4. How do you relax after work?

5. What is your role as instructional leader?

6. What is your role as operational leader?

7. Should a principal be personally involved in strategic leadership?

8. How might we judge your sense of ethics?

9. To what extent would you collaborate with others?

10. How and why would you involve community participation in your school?

11. How would you resolve personnel conflicts?

12. Under what circumstances would you rate a teacher "unsatisfactory"?

13. What motivates you?

14. Why have you applied for this position?

15. Would others consider you to be a courageous leader?

16. Describe a poor decision you've made.

17. What are your limitations?

18. Under what circumstances, if any, would you seek assistance?

19. How do you envision the role of the superintendent?

20. Does a principal have to have been a good teacher to serve as a principal?

21. Describe three concrete ways you would involve parents at your school.

22. Describe your schoolwide discipline plan.

23. Have you written grants? If so, explain.

24. How would you encourage multicultural education and diversity in your school?

25. What impact do you as principal have on student achievement?

26. What opportunities would you offer girls in science and math in your school?

27. What is the role of physical education?

28. Do you believe in the arts? If so, describe how you'd integrate them into the curriculum.

29. How would you collaborate with a local college?

30. Where do you see yourself in 20 years?

Part I

Book One:
What Every Principal Should Know About Instructional Leadership

Overview of Instructional Leadership:
Inspire Schoolwide Instructional Excellence

Among the numerous factors that influence student learning, quality instruction is at the heart. However, in the face of administrative duties, logistical tasks, and disciplinary responsibilities, many principals struggle with how to efficiently and effectively fulfill their critical role as the school's primary instructional leader.

This concise yet comprehensive guide, representing the first book in the series, outlines an easy-to-implement blueprint for spearheading instructional excellence to bolster student and teacher performance. It offers a proactive approach for setting and attaining high academic goals and boils down the best practices for enhancing teaching, curriculum, supervision, assessment, and professional development.

From the latest research to real-life scenarios, this volume shares tangible strategies for mentoring and meaningfully engaging teachers to maximize instructional prowess and student achievement. Highlights include:

- "Before We Get Started" questionnaire and response analysis (TAKE THE SURVEY NOW on pages xiii–xiv.)
- Case study and accompanying reflective questions (READ THE CASE STUDY NOW and answer the reflective questions on pages 8–11.)
- "What You Should Know About" section framing each chapter
- Self-assessment resource for determining effectiveness of instructional leaders
- Twenty-six best practice behaviors for principal leadership

Best Practices in Teaching

Overview

This chapter in the book covers 10 major concepts that provide a basis from which to engage teachers in discussions and activities concerning instructional improvement. Although principals need not have been "star" teachers, they must, in this author's view, have had significant and successful experiences as classroom teachers. Most fundamentally, they must appreciate that effective schooling begins and ends in the classroom. Principals must feel comfortable in engaging teachers at all levels of experience in workshops and professional development activities aimed to promote excellence in teaching. Effective principals as instructional leaders should know something about each of these areas that have an impact on teaching:

- **Reflective Practice**—is a process by which instructional leaders take the time to contemplate and assess the instructional needs of their schools, identify problem areas, and develop strategies for becoming more effective.
- **Preplanning**—occurs when teachers actively consider learning objectives and other preparatory lesson activities.
- **Allocated, Instructional, Engaged, and Success Time**—are crucial factors in promoting student learning.
- **Wait Time**—increases the amount of time students have to think before responding.
- **Direct Teaching**—refers to the time spent in actual teaching as opposed to non-teaching activities (e.g., collecting assignments).
- **Literacy Development** (including **Reciprocal Teaching**)—is essential regardless of what subject is taught.
- **Differentiated Instruction**—refers to the varied teaching strategies employed by teachers to address the learning needs of all students.
- **Divergent Questioning**—encourages deep and critical thinking.
- **Self-Assessment**—occurs when teachers begin to reflect or see themselves teaching.
- **Constructivism**—refers to learning by doing or active learning.

Discussion Questions

1. How effective were you as a teacher?

2. How can you utilize your experiences in the classroom to facilitate instructional improvement in the school?

3. What resources would you generate to support teaching in your school?

4. How would you plan establishing a school environment that supports teaching excellence?

5. How would you plan on setting aside time for teachers (and yourself and other administrators) to practice reflection?

6. Would you check the book plan for all teachers in your school? Explain.

7. What activities or structures could you establish to facilitate pre-planning among teachers of the same grade, for instance?

8. What is the relationship among allocated, instructional, engaged, and success time? (See Section 3 of the chapter.)

9. Why is wait time so critical for teacher success?

10. How can you ensure that maximum time is spent on direct teaching in the classroom?

11. How might you encourage literacy across the curriculum? (See Section 6 of the chapter.)

12. How do you convince teachers that they can indeed accommodate for differing abilities in the same classroom by differentiating instruction?

13. Research demonstrates that too much time in class is spent on convergent questioning. How would you encourage more use of divergent questioning, especially in cases in which teachers claim, "Students simply can't think"?

14. How would you encourage teachers to critically reflect on their own teaching rather than waiting for your "judgment" or evaluation?

15. A teacher tells you, "Constructivism is inappropriate for my kids." How do you respond? (See Section 10 of the chapter.)

Engagement Activity

Time: 30–40 minutes

Materials: chart paper, markers, masking tape, *What Every Principal Should Know About Instructional Leadership* by Jeffrey Glanz

Refer to the "What You Should Know About Teaching" section on pages 13–14. Divide the group into four smaller groups. Post a piece of chart paper on a wall near where each group is meeting. Have group members assign a recorder. After 20 minutes of group work, reconvene and have each group report out. Compile one list, drawing from each group report, which addresses the five main categories in the following case:

> As principal, you realize that promoting teaching excellence is your foremost responsibility. You are the principal of a relatively small school with an overwhelming number of teachers who have been teaching less than three years. How would you go about promoting an environment that encourages sharing of teaching strategies? Articulate a plan that includes well-defined goals. Discuss in detail three specific strategies you would employ. Which areas of teaching would you focus on? How would you address the 10 key concepts and ideas highlighted in this chapter? What other teaching ideas not discussed in the chapter would you highlight? Finally, how would you assess program effectiveness?

1. Overall Plan:

2. Goals:

3. Specific Strategies:

4. Key Concepts:

5. Assessment:

As a follow-up activity, ask teachers in your school which aspects of teaching they would like to learn more about. What types of professional development activities would they most welcome?

Best Practices in Curriculum

Overview

This chapter in the book covers seven basic aspects of curriculum development that will help principals promote successful instruction. Although principals either need to have been or must become curriculum specialists, successful principals are involved in some of the following, among other, best practices:

- Reviewing all instructional resources and materials in various content areas (e.g., reading and mathematics)
- Aligning teaching with curriculum
- Encouraging teachers and others to review curriculum guidelines and recommend revisions to the instructional program
- Integrating local, state, or national standards into curriculum and instruction
- Reviewing testing and assessment procedures
- Inviting curriculum specialists from within and outside of the school to help facilitate curriculum revisions and development

This chapter suggests that principals know:

- **The Curriculum Development Process**—"involves analysis, design, implementation, and evaluation of educational experiences in a school in order to establish goals, plan experiences, select content, and assess outcomes of school programs" (Wiles & Bondi, 1998, p. 12).
- **Tripod View of Curriculum**—involves three ways of conceiving curriculum: based on the needs of the learner, needs of society, or the knowledge base.
- **Essentialism, Progressivism, and Constructivism**—are three approaches or philosophies to guide curriculum development.
- **The Tyler (1949) Model**—involves four steps to consider in developing curriculum (one model among many others).
- **Planning, Implementing, and Assessing Teaching Learning**—involves a three-step curriculum framework.
- **Designing Quality Curriculum**—involves three guidelines offered by Glatthorn (2000) for designing quality curriculum.
- **Using Curriculum Standards**—involves attending to local, state, professional, and national standards to ensure quality learning.

Discussion Questions

1. What did you learn about curriculum development when you were in graduate school?

2. What have you learned about curriculum "on the job"?

3. What would you say to a fellow principal who argues that curriculum "should be left to curriculum specialists"?

4. How can your knowledge of curriculum facilitate instructional improvement in the school?

5. What resources would you generate to support curriculum development in your school?

6. How would you involve teachers in curriculum development?

7. How would you respond to a teacher who argues, "Why are we involved since the curriculum is already so fixed by the state and reinforced by rigorous standards?"

8. Referring to Section 2 "Understand the Three Types of Curriculum" in the chapter, how can the information about the Tripod View of Curriculum assist you in better answering the previous question?

9. Do you believe in constructivist approaches to curriculum and instruction? (See Section 3 in the chapter.)

10. What activities or structures could you establish to facilitate curriculum development among teachers of the same grade, for instance?

11. What is the relationship among planning, implementing, and assessing teaching and learning? (See Section 5 in the chapter.)

12. How might you assist a new teacher in balancing teaching a special unit of interest to her with the fact that she must "cover" other required areas of curriculum?

13. How might you use the technology standards in the chapter to promote best practice in technology in a particular grade or even schoolwide?

Engagement Activity

Time: 30–40 minutes

Materials: Figure 3.2 in the chapter, chart paper, markers, masking tape, *What Every Principal Should Know About Instructional Leadership* by Jeffrey Glanz

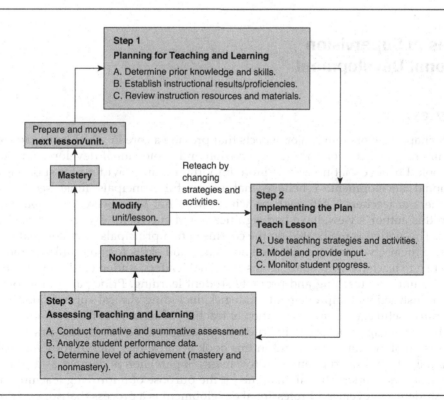

Operationalizing the Steps in Developing the Curriculum

SOURCE: From Don M. Beach & Judy Reinhartz. *Supervisory Leadership: Focus on Instruction,* Published by Allyn & Bacon, Boston, MA. Copyright © 2000 by Pearson Education. Reprinted by permission of the publisher.

Refer to the "Understand the Curriculum Development Process" section on pages 42–44. Divide the group into four smaller groups. Post a piece of chart paper on a wall near where each group is meeting. Have group members assign a recorder. After 15 minutes of group work, reconvene and have each group report out. Compile one list, drawing from each group report, which addresses the four main categories in the following case:

As a principal you want to encourage teachers to think creatively about instruction and utilize curriculum to develop innovative approaches to teaching in the classroom. You are the principal of a large middle school with teachers of varying levels of experience. How would you go about promoting an environment that encourages curriculum development? Using Figure 3.2, go through each of the three steps by identifying a curriculum area of interest to the group. Discuss at least one specific strategy you would employ for each step.

1. Overarching area of curriculum to be addressed:

2. Step 1: Specific strategy employed:

3. Step 2: Specific strategy employed:

4. Step 3: Specific strategy employed:

As a follow-up activity, brainstorm with colleagues the ways in which they "enliven" curriculum while simultaneously meeting the "standards-driven" curriculum.

Best Practices in Supervision and Professional Development

Overview

This chapter covers four major aspects that provide a core in which to engage teachers in meaningful practices concerning supervision and professional development. As noted in the book, I believe that no area is more important than providing for supervision and professional development. I believe that successful principals must see themselves as "teachers of teachers." Although principals need not have been "star" teachers, they must, in this author's view, have had significant and successful experiences as classroom teachers. This notion is predicated on the condition that principals have adequate teaching experience themselves and possess the knowledge and skills to communicate good teaching practice to teachers. Principals, as instructional leaders, understand how to work with teachers to improve teaching and promote student learning. Principals can incorporate a variety of instructional-improvement strategies, including clinical supervision that incorporates purposeful classroom observation of teachers in action, not for evaluative purposes but, rather, to engage teachers in instructional dialogue about classroom practice. In fact, no discussion of evaluation is found in this book because the chief purpose of evaluation is accountability, not instructional improvement. Supervision is defined as a process that engages teachers in instructional dialogue for the purpose of improving teaching and promoting student achievement. Professional development is a process that supports ongoing and effective supervision. Effective principals, as instructional leaders, should know something about each of these areas that have an impact on teaching:

- **Clinical Supervision**—is a cyclical process of engaging teachers in instructional dialogue based on three basic stages: planning, observing, and analysis or reflection.
- **Action Research**—occurs when principals encourage teachers to think about their teaching and student learning in systematic ways by employing the scientific method: identify a question or problem, pose research questions, gather and analyze data, interpret results, derive conclusions, and take action to improve practice.
- **Professional Development**—is a process of supporting teachers' work and student learning by systematic, continuous, meaningful, and knowledge-based workshops and seminars about collaboratively developed topics.
- **PCPOWBIRDS**—All good principals work with teachers on instructional activities that include planning, observations, workshops, sharing bulletins and research, inter-visitations, providing resources, demo lessons, and staff development.

Discussion Questions

1. How effective were you as a teacher?

2. How can you utilize your experiences in the classroom to facilitate instructional improvement in the school?

3. Do you agree with the aforementioned definitions of supervision and professional development?

4. How do you find the time to engage teachers in meaningful discussions about instruction?

5. Do you separate supervision from evaluation? Explain.

6. How do you deal with a teacher who has recently entered your school from another district who has had a very poor experience with supervision? She resists your attempts at "instructional dialogue."

7. What resources would you generate to support professional development?

8. To what extent would you involve teachers in planning for and implementing professional development?

9. How would you involve the most experienced, tenured teachers in the supervision or professional development process?

10. A colleague reports that clinical supervision "simply takes too much time." "I prefer," he says, "a check-list approach to supervision." How do you respond?

11. What did supervision "look like" in the school in which you served as a teacher?

12. What did professional development "look like" in the school in which you served as a teacher?

13. What is the role of the principal in supervision? In professional development?

14. What is the role of the assistant principal in supervision? In professional development?

15. How do your roles complement one another and/or differ?

16. Does a coach "do" supervision, rather than you or the Assistant Principal in your school? Explain.

17. What does action research have to do with supervision? (See Section 2 in the chapter.)

18. How would you encourage teachers to use action research to improve instruction?

19. Describe the ideal professional development program. What would it take for such an ideal to take place in your school?

20. How might PCPOWBIRDS assist your efforts in supervision? (See Section 4 in the chapter.)

Engagement Activity

Time: 60–90 minutes

Materials: Copy of the Key Steps—Directive Informational Approach, Collaborative Approach, and Self-Directed Approach on pages 71–72 of *What Every Principal Should Know About Instructional Leadership* by Jeffrey Glanz. Additional resources might include "crib sheets" from *Supervision That Improves Teaching: Strategies and Techniques* (2005) by Susan Sullivan and Jeffrey Glanz and a copy of the accompanying video titled "Supervision in Practice."

Refer to the "Implement Clinical Supervision" section on pages 56–72. Divide the group into three smaller groups. Ask them to review the supervisory guidelines on pages 56–72. If the videotape is available, show them excerpts. Have two group members role-play each of the approaches to supervision while the third person serves as observer, noting interactions and taking notes for feedback later. Either go through a complete supervisory cycle or identify one phase in the cycle on which to focus. Ask the observer to provide feedback on the effectiveness of the approach utilized. Change roles among group members. Use reporting out at the end, but also from time to time to raise or underscore certain points.

Try to encourage one group to volunteer to have itself videotaped for whole group playback and discussion. This is a great way to highlight and review the supervision process and really build skills. Several 60-minute sessions can be repeated from time to time to reinforce skill development.

Again, if the "Supervision in Practice" video is available, show it to the group and have them ascertain subtle differences among supervisory approaches used with neophyte, intermediate, and more experienced teachers.

As a follow-up activity, have participants continue their practice over time. Have them role-play once more and share how the skill levels have improved.

Best Practices in Promoting Student Achievement

Overview

This concluding chapter highlights 26 best leadership principal behaviors that have been proven to positively affect student achievement. Although other forms of leadership are important, without mindful attention to instructional leadership, principals will not be able to accomplish their ultimate goal; that is, improving student learning and achievement. The 26 behaviors are noted here:
Effective principals:

- Establish a safe and orderly school environment by communicating high expectations for student behavior. (You can't have high student achievement in a chaotic environment in which student misbehavior is tolerated.)
- Articulate a vision that includes clear goals for student learning.
- Communicate high expectations for student achievement. (You also must encourage teachers to demonstrate their belief that all students can achieve.)

- Persevere despite setbacks. (Student achievement doesn't occur linearly; sometimes, actually most often, students may falter academically until a breakthrough occurs; good principals understand this fact and don't panic.)
- Maintain a high profile. (Effective principals are always available to support teachers instructionally.)
- Support positive school climate by encouraging and nurturing a caring school.
- Communicate the importance of instructional excellence.
- Attend to the personal and emotional needs of students and teachers.
- Reach out to parents and community for assistance with both instruction and school governance.
- Demonstrate their commitment to instructional excellence through symbolic leadership (e.g., one principal vowed to shave his head if student achievement in reading rose more than one grade level schoolwide. I am not, of course, recommending you follow suit, but do realize the importance of symbolic actions).
- Encourage participative decision making with teachers and staff regarding instructional issues.
- Support a cooperative schoolwide learning environment.
- Actively and continuously engage in instructional matters and decisions.
- Actively and continuously engage others in instructional matters and decisions.
- Establish a norm of continuous improvement by continually pushing for improvement in student performance.
- Engage faculty in instructional and curricular matters at every turn.
- Visit classrooms frequently, observing and providing feedback continuously (Downey et al., 2004).
- Respect teacher autonomy and do not excessively intrude.
- Support teacher risk taking, in which teachers try out innovative instructional strategies.
- Secure ample instructional resources (personnel or otherwise) to implement professional development.
- Avoid administrative intrusions such as loudspeaker announcements.
- Monitor student academic progress systematically.
- Interpret performance data and use such data to make instructional improvements.
- Acknowledge the accomplishments of faculty in terms of their hard work to improve student performance and to recognize students for their individual achievements.
- "Walk the talk" (i.e., effective principals don't just talk about improving instruction, they take specific actions that demonstrate their commitment to instruction).
- Avoid bureaucratic or autocratic practices that stifle teacher autonomy.

Discussion Questions

1. Do you really believe that the principal has the greatest impact on student achievement? Explain.

2. What behaviors have you seen in exemplary principals that positively affected student learning and achievement?

3. Conversely, describe behaviors that had the opposite affect. What can you learn from them, besides simply avoiding them?

4. How would you plan to promote high achievement for all students?

5. Is it realistic to expect that all students achieve high?

6. What would you need as a principal to ensure high achievement for all students?

7. What specific strategies would you employ in working with beginning teachers?

8. What specific strategies would you use with tenured but burned out teachers?

Engagement Activity

Time: 30 minutes

Materials: List of 26 behaviors printed here and a copy of *What Every Principal Should Know About Instructional Leadership* by Jeffrey Glanz

Refer to the "Promoting Student Achievement for All" chapter on pages 91–94. An additional resource might be *School Leadership That Works* by Robert Marzano and colleagues (2005). Have participants work independently and then pair-and-share, until the group facilitator brings the group together for a brainstorming session. Have participants carefully read the list of 26 behaviors and then answer these questions:

1. Select the five behaviors you think might have the greatest impact on student achievement and explain why.

2. What specific strategy would you recommend to ensure that each of the five behaviors you previously selected was successful?

3. What principal behavior is not listed that should be listed?

4. Compare Cotton's list on pages 92–93 with the list by Marzano and colleagues (2001). What behaviors did Marzano identify that Cotton did not? Do they make sense? Explain.

5. Describe a principal you know (or knew) who did something (describe) that demonstrably had a positive effect on achievement? How do you know (the evidence)?

As a follow-up activity, survey principals to determine what they do that best promotes student achievement. They should be able to provide evidence to support their statements.

Culminating Activity

Time: 60–90 minutes

Materials: This culminating activity utilizes Resources A and B in *What Every Principal Should Know About Instructional Leadership* by Jeffrey Glanz.

Divide the participants into two groups. One group will work on Resource A and the other group will work on Resource B. Make sure to provide copies of each Resource to each group (only one copy for each group, not one copy for each group member because the group participation of all members will be enhanced by giving only one copy for the group). Allow groups to assign responsibilities to members:

Recorder—person responsible for recording info for group

Monitor—ensures that each group member participates (e.g., in the case of a silent member, the monitor might ask, "Steve, what do you think?" or "Do we all agree on the solution?")

Captain—ensures group stays on task to complete assigned task

Reporter—reports out to large group at end of session (may be one or two individuals)

What other roles/responsibilities can you encourage?

Resource A

Select as many in-basket simulations as time permits and brainstorm three specific strategies for coping/dealing with each scenario. Ensure all group members agree on each strategy (prioritize them here as relevant to participants). During the report out phase, rather than just reading the scenario and reporting strategies, the group should first encourage audience reaction and participation and then share group strategies.

Resource B

Members administer the survey to the entire group. In other words, all session participants take the survey anonymously. Group members then tabulate results for a later presentation and discussion. Afterwards, Resource B group members offer their personal insights to questionnaire items. For instance, someone might share that she doesn't really feel comfortable giving workshops to teachers in a particular area. Discussion should occur within a collegial, non-threatening, and supportive environment that encourages alternate ways of seeing things and offers positive, constructive suggestions. Group members, during the reporting out session, should plan, in advance, key questions to provoke audience participation.

Instructional Leadership Reproducibles

Reproducible #1. Questionnaire

Directions: Using the following Likert scale, circle the answer that best represents your on-the-spot belief about each statement.

SA = Strongly Agree ("For the most part, yes.")
A = Agree ("Yes, but . . .")
D = Disagree ("No, but . . .")
SD = Strongly Disagree ("For the most part, no.")

SA   A   D   SD   1. To be effective, the principal must have been a successful classroom teacher.

SA   A   D   SD   2. Good principals must know how to facilitate best practices in teaching, curriculum, and supervision.

SA   A   D   SD   3. It is reasonable to expect a principal to serve as a presenter in a professional development session.

SA   A   D   SD   4. It is reasonable to expect principals to know as much or more about wait time, Bloom's Taxonomy, and differentiated instruction than teachers.

SA   A   D   SD   5. It is reasonable to expect principals to lead disciplinary instruction in mathematics, biology, English, history, and so forth.

SA   A   D   SD   6. The principal should spend many hours in the classroom each day.

SA   A   D   SD   7. The principal should be the most important instructional leader in a school.

SA   A   D   SD   8. The principal is the single greatest factor in determining the extent of student achievement.

SA   A   D   SD   9. Instructional leadership should take priority over other forms of leadership.

SA   A   D   SD   10. I am comfortable facilitating instructional leadership in my school.

Reproducible #2. Quotations

Examine these quotations on the importance of an instructional leader: What do they mean to you?

"A school learning community must hold curriculum, instruction, and assessment central to its work if it expects to make a difference for student learning. The principal's role has evolved from manager to instructional leader to facilitator-leader of the school learning community. Through collaborative work of the principal and teachers, curriculum development and instructional and assessment practices continually change to conform to the needs of all students. Curriculum, instruction, and assessment are the heart of the school learning community. The role of the principal is to facilitate and keep the school focused on excellent curriculum, instruction, and assessment to meet students' learning needs and improve achievement."

—Marsha Speck

"The key factor to the individual school's success is the building principal, who sets the tone as the school's educational leader."

—Arthur Anderson

"The principals of tomorrow's schools must be instructional leaders who possess the requisite skills, capacities, and commitment to lead the accountability parade, not follow it. Excellence in school leadership should be recognized as the most important component of school reform. Without leadership, the chances for systemic improvement in teaching and learning are nil."

—Gerald N. Tirozzi

"Good principals make good teaching and learning possible."

—From Robert D. Ramsey, *501 Ways to Boost Your Child's Success in School*

"The most important person in the school is the principal."

—Hillary Rodham Clinton

"Never underestimate the importance of instructional leadership. . . . Effective principals do not allow managerial tasks to consume their days. They create adequate time to focus on being the instructional leaders of their schools. It is the key part of their job."

—Paul G. Young

"Effective school leadership, in the form of a dedicated, skilled principal, is a key element in creating and maintaining high quality schools."

—Philip A. Cusick

"Before I stepped into my first classroom as a teacher, I thought teaching was mainly instruction, partly performing, certainly being in front and at the center of classroom life. Later, with much chaos and some pain, I learned that this is the least of it—teaching includes a more splendorous range of actions. Teaching is instructing, advising, counseling, organizing, assessing, guiding, goading, showing, managing, modeling, coaching, disciplining, prodding, preaching, persuading, proselytizing, listening, interacting, nursing, and inspiring."

—Gloria Ladson-Billings

"Each leader is responsible for ensuring that the students entrusted to his or her care receive a first-class education in all of the core curriculum areas."

—Rod Paige

"Supervision is and always will be the key to the high instructional standards of America's public schools."

—Harold Spears

"The goal of supervision is to facilitate the process of teaching and learning through a multitude of approaches that can encompass curriculum and staff development, action research, and peer, self-, and student assessment. . . . Supervision is the process of engaging teachers in instructional dialogue for the purpose of improving teaching and increasing student achievement."

—Susan Sullivan and Jeffrey Glanz

"Too often, professional development is not carefully conceived to help teachers develop and use specific skills needed to increase student achievement. Also, most professional development is not rigorously evaluated to determine what teachers learned and how effectively they applied that learning in their schools and classrooms. As educators heed the call for a research-based approach to professional development, they must redesign their programs to provide an effective system of instructional support for teachers. This new approach to professional development must be linked to concrete teaching tasks, organized around problem solving, informed by research, and sustained over time."

—Gene R. Carter

"A key difference between highly effective and less effective principals is that the former are actively involved in the curricular and instructional life of their schools."

—Kathleen Cotton

Reproducible #3. Three Research-Based Findings About the Activities of an Effective Instructional Leader

Committed to instructional leadership, good principals know, among other things, the following:

1. The single greatest influence on students in a classroom is the teacher. "Teachers have a powerful, long-lasting influence on their students" (Stronge, 2002, p. vii). Good principals support good teachers by providing instructional services and resources on a continuous basis. Moreover, good principals attract and hire certified teachers who have specific knowledge, skills, and dispositions that are essential to promote student achievement; certified teachers are more successful than unlicensed teachers. Good principals also realize that retaining good teachers is essential because experience counts. "Experienced teachers differ from rookie teachers in that they have attained expertise through real-life experiences, classroom practice, and time" (Stronge, 2002, p. 9). Research demonstrates that teachers with more experience, in comparison to inexperienced teachers, plan better, apply a wider range of teaching strategies, more thoroughly understand students' learning needs, and better organize instruction. Good principals understand this research.

2. An emphasis on academics is crucial. Effective principal instructional leaders spend much time discussing the instructional program with colleagues, teachers, parents, students, and district office leaders. They use every available opportunity to discuss instruction: personal informal and formal contacts with teachers, memoranda, e-mail communications, grade and faculty conferences, assembly programs, parent meetings, and so forth. They realize that establishing an orderly environment conducive to educational excellence is necessary. Good principals set high expectations and standards for success (Squires, Huitt, & Segars, 1984). In addition, and more specifically related to instructional improvement, effective principals:

- Establish clearly defined academic goals for the school (by grade).
- Collaboratively develop clear and consistent schoolwide instructional policies.
- Examine instructional grouping patterns to ensure student mastery of content.
- Ensure that instructional time is protected (more on time on task later in Chapter 1, but good principals make sure to minimize intrusions e.g., excessive announcements over the loudspeaker, intrusive attendance report collection by office monitors, etc., which interrupt and compromise classroom teaching and learning).
- Monitor adherence to local or state standards in the curriculum.
- Maintain a systematic method of assessment procedures.
- Review data collected as a result of implementation of an assessment system.
- Share and use the data to help improve the instructional school program.
- Observe teachers and students engaged in the learning process.
- Involve teachers in curriculum planning and decision making.
- Assist teachers who are having instructional difficulties.
- Provide for meaningful, ongoing, collaboratively developed professional development opportunities.

3. The three primary elements of successful instructional leadership are as follows (Blase & Blase, 2004):
   a. Conducting instructional conferences is a primary element of successful instructional leadership. Whether involved in pre- or post-observation conferences, informal or more formal grade conferences, and so on, principals, according to Blase and Blase (2004), exhibit these behaviors: make suggestions, give feedback, model, use inquiry, and solicit opinions from teachers.

b. Providing staff development is a second primary element of successful instructional leadership. According to Blase and Blase (2004),

> Behaviors associated with providing staff development include emphasizing the study of teaching and learning, support for collaboration, development of coaching relationships, use of action research, provision of resources, and application of the principles of adult growth and development to all phases of the staff development program. (p. 162)

c. Developing teacher reflection is a third primary element of successful instructional leadership. Principals purposefully engage teachers in articulating feelings, sharing attitudes, and thinking deeply about instructional issues.

Reproducible #4. Questionnaire on Curriculum

Respond

SA = Strongly Agree ("For the most part, yes.")
A = Agree ("Yes, but . . .")
D = Disagree ("No, but . . .")
SD = Strongly Disagree ("For the most part, no.")

SA   A   D   SD   1. I see my role as principal to provide leadership in implementing state and district standards.

SA   A   D   SD   2. I have a firm understanding of basic curriculum theory.

SA   A   D   SD   3. I understand the connection between the purpose of education and curriculum development.

SA   A   D   SD   4. I cannot help teachers in areas of curriculum, because I am chiefly a manager good at administration, not curriculum.

SA   A   D   SD   5. The knowledge base or content of a curriculum is more important than the needs of the learner.

SA   A   D   SD   6. I am a progressive curriculum thinker and doer who believes in constructivist thought and practice.

SA   A   D   SD   7. I know how to implement the Tyler Rationale.

SA   A   D   SD   8. I can lead teachers in developing curriculum.

SA   A   D   SD   9. I work with teachers on an ongoing basis to develop new ways to create meaningful curricula.

SA   A   D   SD   10. I fully understand the history of standards-based reform initiatives in this country.

Reproducible #5. Three Approaches to Supervision

Key Steps—Directive Informational Approach

1. Identify the problem or goal and solicit clarifying information.

2. Offer solutions. Ask for the teacher's input into the alternatives offered and request additional ideas.

3. Summarize chosen alternatives, ask for confirmation, and request that the teacher restate final choices.

4. Set a follow-up plan and meeting.

Key Steps—Self-Directed Approach

1. Listen carefully to the teacher's initial statement.

2. Reflect back your understanding of the problem.

3. Constantly clarify and reflect until the real problem is identified.

4. Have the teacher problem-solve and explore consequences of various actions.

5. Have the teacher commit to a decision and firm up a plan.

6. Restate the teacher's plan and set a follow-up meeting.

Key Steps—Collaborative Approach

1. Identify the problem from the teacher's perspective, soliciting as much clarifying information as possible.

2. Reflect back what you've heard for accuracy.

3. Begin collaborative brainstorming, asking the teacher for his or her ideas first.

4. Problem-solve through a sharing and discussion of options.

5. Agree on a plan and follow-up meeting.

Reproducible #6. What Effective Principals Do to Promote Instruction

Effective principals:

- Establish a safe and orderly school environment by communicating high expectations for student behavior. (You can't have high student achievement in a chaotic environment in which student misbehavior is tolerated.)
- Articulate a vision that includes clear goals for student learning.
- Communicate high expectations for student achievement. (You also must encourage teachers to demonstrate their belief that all students can achieve.)
- Persevere despite setbacks. (Student achievement doesn't occur linearly; sometimes, actually most often, students may falter academically until a breakthrough occurs; good principals understand this fact and don't panic.)
- Maintain a high profile. (Effective principals are always available to support teachers instructionally.)
- Support positive school climate by encouraging and nurturing a caring school.
- Communicate the importance of instructional excellence.
- Attend to the personal and emotional needs of students and teachers.
- Reach out to parents and community for assistance with both instruction and school governance.
- Demonstrate their commitment to instructional excellence through symbolic leadership (e.g., one principal vowed to shave his head if student achievement in reading rose more than one grade level schoolwide. I am not, of course, recommending you follow suit, but do realize the importance of symbolic actions).
- Encourage participative decision making with teachers and staff regarding instructional issues.
- Support a cooperative schoolwide learning environment.
- Actively and continuously engage in instructional matters and decisions.
- Actively and continuously engage others in instructional matters and decisions.
- Establish a norm of continuous improvement by continually pushing for improvement in student performance.
- Engage faculty in instructional and curricular matters at every turn.
- Visit classrooms frequently, observing and providing feedback continuously (Downey et al., 2004).
- Respect teacher autonomy and do not excessively intrude.
- Support teacher risk taking, in which teachers try out innovative instructional strategies.
- Secure ample instructional resources (personnel or otherwise) to implement professional development.
- Avoid administrative intrusions such as loudspeaker announcements.
- Monitor student academic progress systematically.
- Interpret performance data and use such data to make instructional improvements.
- Acknowledge the accomplishments of faculty in terms of their hard work to improve student performance and to recognize students for their individual achievements.
- "Walk the talk" (i.e., effective principals don't just talk about improving instruction, they take specific actions that demonstrate their commitment to instruction).
- Avoid bureaucratic or autocratic practices that stifle teacher autonomy.

Reproducible #7. Conclusion:
Making Time for Instructional Leadership

1. *Locate, listen to, and articulate your inner voice.* To quote Fullan and Hargreaves (1996):

> Often, when we say we have no time for something, it's an evasion. What we mean is we have more immediate or convenient things to do with that time. Of course, bulletin boards and visual aids are important. But doing them doesn't make you feel personally uncomfortable. It isn't disquieting. It isn't a personal challenge. Listening to our inner voice is. It requires not just time, but courage and commitment too. (pp. 65–66)

2. *Believe that you can make a difference.* Principals must believe that they can make a difference (Denham & Michael, 1981).

Reproducible #8. Realities of Instructional Leadership: In-Basket Simulations

During an interview you are asked to respond to the following scenarios (first three bullets):

• React to the following statements: *Certainly instructional improvement is necessary. Not all principals, though, are "super" teachers. Rather, a good principal knows how to select other instructional leaders. The role of the principal is to oversee their job and ensure that enough time is spent on instructional improvement.*

• What would you do to encourage teachers to trust that you are there to "help" them and not merely to "evaluate" them?

• How would you forge a role for yourself as an instructional leader and not merely a manager, especially in a school in which the former principal did not focus on instruction?

• The former principal was an administrator type, not an instructional leader. Your faculty is used to the traditional method of evaluation. How would you establish a culture supportive of clinical supervisory practice? Be specific.

• You are a newly assigned principal in a K–5 elementary school. The superintendent has indicated that she is not pleased with the results of the instructional program being provided to children who have been held over because of their lack of progress in class work and their poor performances on standardized reading and math tests. The held-over children are placed together in the same class in the grade. The superintendent requests that you review the situation and make recommendations to her. Describe with justifications four recommendations you would submit to the superintendent for improving the instructional program for these held-over children so that they can function more effectively in the school.

• You are a principal at a local high school that has an excellent reputation for its rigorous curriculum. You receive an anonymous note in your mailbox informing you that Mr. O'Hare is teaching topics that are not part of the prescribed history curriculum and that students will not be prepared for the statewide competency exam. Assuming that the allegations are verified, describe your actions.

• You are assigned as a principal in a middle school in an urban area in which teachers complain that they are unable to teach their subject area because of the students' poor reading skills. Outline the steps you would take in dealing with the teachers and in improving the reading abilities of the students. Include the techniques, services, and personnel you would utilize. Discuss the curriculum development initiatives you would take.

• Explain how you would use your schoolwide assessment system to improve instruction in general. More specifically, let's say that your data indicate that students are ill prepared to use technology in meaningful, educational ways. What would you do to ensure that all students are "technologically" competent?

• You are passionate about inclusive practice and want to increase the number of inclusion classes in your school. Some vocal parents inform you that they will resist such an increase, because they don't want their children's education jeopardized by having special education students in the same classroom as their children. Explain the steps you might take to develop more meaningful inclusive practices in your school and describe how you would ensure high achievement for all students in your school in general?

Reproducible #9. Assessing Your Role as Instructional Leader

SA = Strongly Agree ("For the most part, yes.")
A = Agree ("Yes, but . . .")
D = Disagree ("No, but . . .")
SD = Strongly Disagree ("For the most part, no.")

Planning and Preparation

SA A D SD   1. Teachers should be offered guidance in planning and preparing for instruction, and I feel comfortable in doing so.

SA A D SD   2. Good teachers should display solid content knowledge and make connections between the parts of their discipline or with other disciplines.

SA A D SD   3. Good teachers should consider the importance of prerequisite knowledge when introducing new topics.

SA A D SD   4. Good teachers actively build on students' prior knowledge and seek causes for students' misunderstanding.

SA A D SD   5. Good teachers are content knowledgeable but may need additional assistance with pedagogical strategies and techniques, and I feel comfortable providing such assistance.

SA A D SD   6. I am familiar with pedagogical strategies and continually search for best practices to share with my teachers.

SA A D SD   7. Good teachers know much about the developmental needs of their students.

SA A D SD   8. Principals are familiar with learning styles and multiple intelligences theories and can help teachers apply them to instructional practice.

SA A D SD   9. I do not fully recognize the value of understanding teachers' skills and knowledge as a basis for their teaching.

SA A D SD   10. Goal setting is critical to teacher success in planning and preparing, and the principal should offer to collaborate with teachers in this area.

SA A D SD   11. I am familiar with curricular and teaching resources to assist teachers.

SA A D SD   12. I know I can help teachers develop appropriate learning activities suitable for students.

SA A D SD   13. I can help teachers plan for a variety of meaningful learning activities matched to school, district, and state instructional goals.

SA   A   D   SD   14. I would encourage teachers to use varied instructional grouping.

SA   A   D   SD   15. I can assist teachers in developing a systematic plan for assessment of student learning.

SA   A   D   SD   16. I can provide professional development for teachers in planning and preparation.

The Classroom Environment

SA   A   D   SD   1. I realize the importance of classroom management and discipline.

SA   A   D   SD   2. I expect that teacher interactions with students are generally friendly and demonstrate warmth and caring.

SA   A   D   SD   3. I expect teachers to develop a system of discipline without my assistance.

SA   A   D   SD   4. I will play an active role in monitoring grade and school discipline plans.

SA   A   D   SD   5. I support the classroom teachers in matters of discipline.

SA   A   D   SD   6. I always communicate the high expectation to all my teachers that they are the most critical element in the classroom.

SA   A   D   SD   7. I expect teachers to have a well-established and well-defined system of rules and procedures.

SA   A   D   SD   8. I expect that teachers are alert to student behavior at all times.

SA   A   D   SD   9. I can provide professional development to teachers on classroom management.

SA   A   D   SD   10. As a teacher, I was a competent classroom manager.

Instruction

SA   A   D   SD   1. I expect that teachers' directions to students will be clear and not confusing.

SA   A   D   SD   2. My directives to teachers about instruction are clear.

SA   A   D   SD   3. My spoken language as a teacher was clear and appropriate according to the grade level of my students.

SA   A   D   SD   4. I believe that teachers' questioning techniques are among the most critical skills needed to promote pupil learning, and I feel comfortable helping teachers frame good questions.

SA   A   D   SD   5. Teacher questions must be of uniformly high quality.

SA   A   D   SD   6. From my experience, teachers mostly lecture (talk) to students without enough student participation.

SA   A   D   SD   7. I encourage teachers to encourage students to participate and prefer for students to take an active role in learning.

SA   A   D   SD   8. I can provide a workshop for teachers on giving assignments that are appropriate to students and that engage students mentally.

SA   A   D   SD   9. I don't know how to group students appropriately for instruction.

SA   A   D   SD   10. I am very familiar with grouping strategies to promote instruction.

SA   A   D   SD   11. I can advise teachers on how best to select appropriate and effective instructional materials and resources.

SA   A   D   SD   12. My demo lessons to teachers are highly coherent, and my pacing is consistent and appropriate.

SA   A   D   SD   13. I rarely provide appropriate feedback to my teachers.

SA   A   D   SD   14. Feedback to my teachers is consistent, appropriate, and of high quality.

SA   A   D   SD   15. I expect my teachers to rely heavily on the teacher's manual for instruction.

SA   A   D   SD   16. I consistently encourage teachers to seek my advice on teaching and learning matters.

SA   A   D   SD   17. I encourage teachers to use wait time effectively.

SA   A   D   SD   18. I feel competent enough to give a workshop to teachers on effective use of wait time.

SA   A   D   SD   19. I consider myself an instructional leader.

SA   A   D   SD   20. Teachers perceive me as an instructional leader.

Professional Responsibilities

SA   A   D   SD   1. I have difficulty assessing the effectiveness of teachers.

SA   A   D   SD   2. I can accurately assess how well I am doing as an instructional leader.

SA   A   D   SD   3. I really don't know how to improve teaching skills.

SA   A   D   SD   4. I am aware of what I need to do in order to become an effective instructional leader.

SA   A   D   SD   5. I rarely encourage parents to become involved in instructional matters.

SA   A   D   SD   6. I actively and consistently encourage parents to visit classrooms.

SA   A   D   SD   7. I feel comfortable giving workshops to parents on curricular and instructional matters.

SA   A   D   SD   8. I have difficulty relating to my colleagues in a cordial and professional manner.

SA   A   D   SD   9. I collaborate with my colleagues in a cordial and professional manner.

SA   A   D   SD   10. I avoid becoming involved in school and district projects.

SA   A   D   SD   11. I rarely encourage teachers to engage in professional development activities.

SA   A   D   SD   12. I seek out opportunities for professional development to enhance my pedagogical skills.

SA   A   D   SD   13. I am rarely alert to teachers' instructional needs.

SA   A   D   SD   14. I serve teachers.

SA   A   D   SD   15. I am an advocate for students' rights.

SA   A   D   SD   16. I am an advocate for teachers' rights.

SA   A   D   SD   17. I rarely encourage teachers to serve on a school-based committee.

SA   A   D   SD   18. I enjoy working with teachers collaboratively on instructional matters.

Part II

Book Two:
What Every Principal Should Know About Cultural Leadership

Overview of Cultural Leadership:
Set the Tone for Schoolwide Success
and Watch Student Achievement Soar

Improved student achievement is cultivated in a safe, stimulating, and cooperative learning environment. This user-friendly guide provides principals ways to focus on creating a positive school climate and culture, realizing visionary leadership, embracing cultural diversity, and promoting school self-renewal.

Both research based and rich with examples, this second volume of a seven-part leadership series will instill confidence in new principals and renew the enthusiasm of veteran administrators. Its straightforward insights and proven best practices make it a one-stop resource for harnessing the power of school culture to boost morale and achievement while fostering a successful learning community schoolwide.

This well-organized resource crystallizes key points for quick access and easy implementation through such features as:

- "Before We Get Started" questionnaire and response analysis (TAKE THE SURVEY NOW on pages xiii–xv.)
- Case study and accompanying reflective questions (READ THE CASE STUDY NOW and answer the reflective questions on pages 13–16.)
- "What You Should Know About" section framing each chapter
- Self-assessment resource for determining effectiveness of cultural leadership

Best Practices in Sustaining Positive Organizational Climate and Culture

Overview

A principal plays a critical role in shaping school culture and affecting climate. This chapter in the book covers four important ways to sustain organizational climate and culture. Effective principals, as cultural leaders, should know something about each of these areas that have an impact on teaching:

- **Building Relationships With Students**—Find ways to involve students in meaningful ways. Encourage them to take pride in your school.
- **Building Relationships With Teachers**—A positive learning culture cannot be nurtured without teacher involvement, nor can there be positive climate without satisfied teachers.
- **Building an Ethic of Caring**—Principals must affirm an ethic of caring as their primary mode of belief and behavior.
- **Building Staff Morale**—Rate your staff morale by having your staff complete the following short survey. Remember, you set the tone for school morale by what you say or do. Remain positive (not Pollyannaish, but confident and optimistic).

Discussion Questions

1. What does cultural leadership mean to you?

2. Doesn't a "culture" of a school exist independently of the principal? Why is the principal so important?

3. How can school climate or culture influence student learning?

4. What is the basic difference between culture and climate?

5. In what ways have you seen other principals promote positive school culture?

6. How can you utilize your experiences to facilitate cultural leadership in the school?

7. Referring to the Seven Research-Based Findings on page 8, in what ways have you seen principals model these research findings?

8. How does high visibility and accessibility affect good school climate?

9. Referring to the bulleted questions on page 18, how would you answer each question?

10. What does an ethic of caring mean to you?

Engagement Activity

Time: 30 minutes

Materials: pen and paper for each participant, chart paper, marker, masking tape, *What Every Principal Should Know About Cultural Leadership* by Jeffrey Glanz

Refer to pages 20–29. Form a large circle with the group. Explain that you will play "telephone." Starting with one of the participants, ask her/him to write down one strategy for "building positive relationships with students." The strategy must be simple, practical, and concise. Pass the paper to the person to the right. This person must write down a second strategy that differs from the first. Then, she or he passes the paper on to the third person who also writes a strategy not previously listed. This continues until a participant says, "pass, I cannot think of another strategy that's not already listed." The paper is then passed until another person says likewise. At that point the facilitator takes the paper and records each written strategy on the chart paper for everyone to see and discuss. The viability of the listed strategies is discussed along with other strategies that are brainstormed by the entire group.

Start the procedure over for "building relationships with teachers." Then, finally, with "building an ethic of caring."

As a follow-up activity, have participants anonymously take the brief survey on pages 29–30. Results may then be tabulated and discussed.

Best Practices in Visionary Leadership

Overview

Essentially, this chapter serves as a guide to develop a principal vision statement. Developing such a vision is critical to success because it reflects principal beliefs and values as well as a guide for all activities conducted in the school. It also serves to inspire others to action around some sort of common purpose or goal. Three related areas are covered in this chapter:

- **Examining Beliefs and Values**—Articulating your beliefs and values is essential in order to frame a vision that is genuine and that can serve to inspire others to success.
- **Composing a Vision Statement**—Vision is developed by asking yourself some key questions that seek to uncover deep-seated beliefs and values.
- **Actualizing Your Vision**—Espousing a vision is not enough; you must put it into practice.

Discussion Questions

1. What is the connection among vision, values (culture), and a sense of mission?

2. How have other principals you've known utilized visionary leadership?

3. Why is affirming a definite set of values and beliefs important for a principal? Provide specific examples. (See Section 1 of the chapter.)

4. Draft a vision statement and refer to Question 3 on page 42. Share responses with a colleague. Why is going through such a process so important?

5. Why is symbolic leadership so important? What's the connection with visionary leadership? (See Section 3 of the chapter.)

Engagement Activity

Time: 30 minutes

Materials: Internet access and a copy of *What Every Principal Should Know About Cultural Leadership* by Jeffrey Glanz

Have the group conduct an Internet search by typing in "principal vision statement." Identify at least three different vision statements and answer these questions:

- What do they have in common?
- In what context is each one used?
- How do they compare to the examples given in the chapter?

Then have the group devise a draft of their own brief vision statements. Have each participant share the vision and how it may assist in leading a school. Open discussion should be encouraged utilizing the "whip-around" technique (i.e., go around the room having one person share at a time, allowing anyone to "pass" but able to report out later on).

As a follow-up activity, have participants read the case on pages 48–50 and react to the reflective questions at the end.

Best Practices in Promoting Cultural Diversity Leadership

Overview

This chapter covers three major concepts that promote an appreciation of cultural diversity. As a cultural leader, the principal must provide a forum to sensitize students and others to the nature of prejudice, intolerance, discrimination, and worse. Effective principals, as cultural leaders, should know something about each of these areas that have an impact on teaching:

- **Encouraging Culturally Relevant Teaching**—Principals believe supporting cultural diversity benefits all students because of the belief that all students can learn, albeit at different paces and in different ways.

- **Debunking Myths About Culturally Relevant Pedagogy**—Principals must dispel misconceptions others have about culturally relevant pedagogy.

- **Leading in Culturally Relevant Ways**—Principals must proactively combat prejudices and take proactive measures to serve as cultural leaders.

Discussion Questions

1. Why is it important for a principal to be concerned with issues of equality and justice?

2. Can a principal, in reality, have much impact on gender bias in society or even in the school?

3. Should a principal advocate for multicultural education? Explain why or why not.

4. What does culturally relevant teaching mean to you? (See Section 1 of the book, *What Every Principal Should Know About Cultural Leadership*.)

5. How can a principal support culturally relevant pedagogy? (See Section 2 of the chapter.)

6. How can a principal lead in culturally relevant ways? (See Section 3 of the chapter.)

7. What is the relationship between cultural leadership and instructional leadership?

Engagement Activity

Time: 40 minutes

Materials: *What Every Principal Should Know About Cultural Leadership* by Jeffrey Glanz

Refer to the section on pages 54–66. Divide group participants and randomly assign them to one of the three main sections of the chapter:

- Encouraging Culturally Relevant Teaching
- Debunking Myths About Culturally Relevant Pedagogy
- Leading in Culturally Relevant Ways

Have each group read the assigned section and discuss each reflective question presented. Have participants react to the information presented providing concrete examples as necessary. Using the guidelines in each section will help the facilitator easily conduct an open discussion session.

As a follow-up activity, have participants research and/or discuss practices they have witnessed that support the goals of cultural leadership. What makes these practices so important and effective?

Best Practices in Fostering Organization Self-Renewal Leadership

Overview

This chapter challenges the reader to view school culture and climate within the context of the school as an organization. Organizational theories provide the context in which to best understand human interactions in schools. Schools as organizations are influenced by significant internal and external forces. Principals must acknowledge these forces and proactively address them. The chapter highlights three challenges principals must confront:

- **Dealing With the Problem of Change**—Principals should understand the opportunities that change can bring. As someone once posited (I paraphrase), change can occur without improvement, but no improvement can occur without change.
- **Dealing With the Problem of Conflict**—Principals realize that conflict is inevitable. Strategies for enhancing communication go a long way toward reducing potentially harmful conflicts.
- **Dealing With the Challenge of Renewal**—Principals are forward looking and always look for ways to improve their organization. Strategies for school renewal are as crucial today as ever.

Discussion Questions

1. Do theories of organization and management really help us better deal with the world of practice as a principal? Explain why or why not.

2. Why is it so important to view the school as an organization?

3. What does Figure 5.1 on page 69 indicate about schools? Draw four major conclusions and back up your insights with practical examples.

4. Why are so many schools unwilling to adapt to change?

5. Cite a case in which a principal you've known resisted organizational innovation. Why do you think she or he offered such resistance?

6. Do principals you know readily acknowledge the pervasiveness of conflict?

7. How do you resolve interpersonal conflicts?

8. What does school renewal mean to you? Provide concrete examples.

9. What is the relationship among change, conflict, and renewal?

Engagement Activity

Time: 40 minutes

Materials: chart paper, markers, masking tape, *What Every Principal Should Know About Cultural Leadership* by Jeffrey Glanz

Divide participants into two groups and distribute a case study to each group. Have the group discuss the case and offer the best solution. Then have groups exchange cases so that after 30 minutes, each group has read and offered a resolution to both cases. As facilitator, allow each group to report out on each case. Challenge groups to discuss alternate ways of dealing with the cases. Record similarities and differences on paper.

Case 1:
    You are the new principal of a local high school in an urban area in which a majority of teachers are tenured with an average of 15 years teaching experience. You want to implement inclusive, collaborative team teaching classrooms, but you are met at every turn by resistance from senior faculty and union officials. What would you do to effect the changes you deem so critical?

Case 2:
    A faculty member approaches another faculty member in her office. He insists that she apologize for remarks he heard that she made against him in the cafeteria. She denies the accusation and asks him to leave her office. He refuses and shouts, "I demand an answer." She attempts to close the door, forcing him to step backwards. He pushes the door back banging her in the hand and head. She screams in pain. He steps back but still demands an explanation. "You're nuts," she shouts. She files charges against him and calls the police. The police reports to the school. You meet them at the door. How do you deal with this situation?
    As a follow-up activity, have participants refer to pages 81–83 and offer ways they can actually accomplish each bulleted item. Require them to provide details and examples.

Culminating Activity

Time: 60–90 minutes

Materials: This culminating activity utilizes Resources A and B in *What Every Principal Should Know About Cultural Leadership* by Jeffrey Glanz.

Divide the participants into two groups. One group will work on Resource A and the other group will work on Resource B. Make sure to provide copies of each Resource to each group (only one for each group, not one copy for each group member because the group participation of all members will be enhanced by giving only one copy for the group). Allow groups to assign responsibilities to members:

Recorder—person responsible for recording info for group

Monitor—ensures that each group member participates (e.g., in the case of a silent member, the monitor might ask, "Steve, what do you think?" or "Do we all agree on the solution?")

Captain—ensures group stays on task to complete assigned task

Reporter—reports out to large group at end of session (may be one or two individuals)

What other roles/responsibilities can you encourage?

Resource A
Select as many in-basket simulations as time permits and brainstorm three specific strategies for coping/dealing with each scenario. Ensure all group members agree on each strategy (prioritize them here as relevant). During the report out phase, rather than just reading the scenario and reporting strategies, the group should first encourage audience reaction and participation and then share group strategies.

Resource B
Members administer the survey to the entire group. In other words, all session participants take the survey anonymously. Group members then tabulate results for later presentation and discussion. Afterwards, Resource B group members offer their personal insights to questionnaire items. For instance, someone might share that she doesn't really feel comfortable giving parents voice in setting school academic goals. Discussion should occur within a collegial, non-threatening, but supportive environment, encouraging alternate ways of seeing things and offering positive, constructive suggestions. During the reporting out session, group members should plan, in advance, key questions to provoke audience participation.

Reproducible #1. Questionnaire

Directions: Using the Likert scale below, circle the answer that best represents your on-the-spot belief about each statement.

SA = Strongly Agree ("For the most part, yes.")
A = Agree ("Yes, but . . .")
D = Disagree ("No, but . . .")
SD = Strongly Disagree ("For the most part, no.")

SA   A   D   SD   1. To be effective, the principal should spend a great deal of time enhancing the culture of the school organization.

SA   A   D   SD   2. Good principals try to build a team spirit in their school.

SA   A   D   SD   3. Examining practices of the former principal is an important task of a new building principal.

SA   A   D   SD   4. I intend to encourage teachers to take initiative in solving schoolwide problems.

SA   A   D   SD   5. I frequently recognize others (i.e., teachers, students, parents, assistant principals) for doing good work.

SA   A   D   SD   6. I believe that shared beliefs and values among faculty and administration lead to positive school climate.

SA   A   D   SD   7. Developing close, friendly, cooperative relations with others is important to me.

SA   A   D   SD   8. I sometimes speak negatively about others when they are not present.

SA   A   D   SD   9. Although I realize that I am the school leader, I also realize that I am not the only leader.

SA   A   D   SD   10. I value and seek advice from others, including teachers.

SA   A   D   SD   11. Conflict in a school or in a grade can be viewed as a means to promote individual and organizational learning and growth.

SA   A   D   SD   12. I seek the advice and input of others in terms of "how I am doing" as a cultural leader.

SA   A   D   SD   13. I believe that schools exist for the children.

SA   A   D   SD   14. A principal determines, in large measure, whether the organizational climate of a school is positive or toxic.

SA   A   D   SD   15. Visionary leadership is solely or largely reserved for the principal.

SA   A   D   SD   16. A leader with vision can accomplish anything.

SA   A   D   SD   17. The principal should champion cultural diversity in the school.

SA   A   D   SD   18. Organizational equilibrium is a major responsibility of the principal.

SA   A   D   SD   19. Developing and sustaining a learning community is a primary aim of the principal.

SA   A   D   SD   20. I really believe that all students can learn and that all teachers can be successful.

Reproducible #2. Cultural Leader's Tasks

A cultural leader is concerned with these areas of leadership, among others:

- Examining learned patterns of behavior via the norms, policies, and procedures of the past and paying close attention to how people are currently interacting and accomplishing their respective tasks
- Realizing the impact of these learned patterns of behaviors on school organization, teacher commitment, staff morale, student achievement, and community involvement
- Understanding that shared values and beliefs founded on participatory democracy, social justice, and individual growth are essential for creating and maintaining a nontoxic learning community
- Supporting, nurturing, and extending a learning environment that encourages critical reflection about commonly held ideas and values
- Leading others to develop shared vision and purpose
- Believing (and acting upon those beliefs) that people can forge shared meanings and successfully achieve their potential
- Affirming cultural diversity by actively combating prejudice and discrimination in every facet of schooling, and cherishing the contributions that each individual can make to the school
- Dealing with change, and even conflict, as natural consequences of one's work, and believing that constructive conflict and positive change can move the organization to higher levels of achievement
- Building and sustaining a learning community that is dynamic, resilient, evolving, and receptive to the learning imperatives of students (Roberts & Pruitt, 2003; Sergiovanni, 1999)

Reproducible #3. Quotations

Examine these quotations on culture and climate. What do they mean to you?

"The educational leader needs to have knowledge of his or her own values and the ability to translate that knowledge into action."
—Paul M. Quick and Anthony H. Normore

"A school's culture and the classroom climate are the direct results of attitudes, behavior, and interactions among teachers, administrators, parents, students, and staff."
—Edward F. DeRoche

"Leadership often involves challenging people to live up to their words, to close the gap between their espoused values and their actual behavior."
—Ronald A. Heifetz and Marty Linsky

"School culture includes values, symbols, beliefs, and shared meanings of parents, students, teachers, and others conceived as a group or community."
—Thomas J. Sergiovanni

"An effective school has a positive school climate. Students feel good about attending such a school and teachers feel good about teaching there. The entire staff works together to foster a caring attitude."
—C. A. Bartell

"The principal is the key player in a school; from the principal, the climate of the school will come. The climate of a school is its moral feeling derived from the values that the principal advocates and makes actionable. The climate significantly impacts the culture. The culture is defined by the practices, both explicit and implicit, in which the constituents of the school are involved. . . . The climate and culture of the school impacts the type of community that a school will be. The sense of community is defined by how the relationships within the school are created, valued, sustained, and managed."
—Paul M. Quick and Anthony H. Normore

"The principal's contribution to the quality of the school climate is arguably a composite of all the things he or she says or does."
—Kathleen Cotton

"The culture of an organization makes clear what the organization stands for—its values, its beliefs, its true (as distinguished from its publicly stated) goals—and provides tangible ways in which individuals in the organization may personally identify with that culture."
—Robert G. Owens

"Multicultural education is a concept that incorporates cultural differences and provides equality in schools. For it to become a reality in the formal school situation, the total environment must reflect a commitment to multicultural education. The diverse cultural backgrounds and microcultural memberships of students and families are as important in developing effective instructional strategies as are their physical and mental capabilities. Further, educators must understand the influence of racism, sexism, classism on the lives of their students and ensure that these are not perpetuated in the classroom [and in the school]."
—Donna M. Gollnick and Philip C. Chinn

"Embarking upon a career in educational leadership requires both a strong sense of purpose and a clear vision if we are to initiate necessary reforms and to help create the magnificent schools our students so richly deserve."
—Patricia Andersen, leadership candidate in New York City

"The self-renewing school possesses three essential characteristics: First, a culture that supports adaptability and responsiveness to change. . . . Second, a set of clear-cut, explicit, and well-known procedures through which participants can engage in . . . collaborative problem-solving. Third, . . . a school that knows when and how to reach out to seek appropriate ideas and resources for use in solving its problems."
—Robert C. Owens

"Learning communities are concerned with growth and continuous self-renewal of both individuals and organizations. The leader is therefore responsible for building organizations where people are continually expanding their capabilities to shape their future—that is, leaders are responsible for learning."
—Gerald C. Ubben, Larry W. Hughes, and Cynthia J. Norris

"Communitas, communis—to find what is held in common or shared by many."
—Latin root of the word *community*

Reproducible #4. Cultural Understandings

Deal and Peterson (1999) recommend several questions that give principals a way to understand a school's culture:

- How long has the school existed?
- Why was it built, and who were the first inhabitants?
- Who has had a major influence on the school's direction?
- What critical incidents occurred in the past, and how were they resolved, if at all?
- What were the preceding principals, teachers, and students like?
- What does the school's architecture convey? How is space arranged and used?
- What subcultures exist inside and outside the school?
- Who are the recognized (and unrecognized) heroes and villains in the school?
- What do people say (and think) when asked what the school stands for? What would they miss if they left?
- What events are assigned special importance?
- How is conflict typically defined? How is it handled?
- What are the key ceremonies and stories of the school?
- What do people wish for? Are there patterns to their individual dreams? (pp. 17–19)

Reproducible #5. Seven Research-Based Findings About the Activities of a Cultural Leader

Committed to cultural leadership, good principals know, among other things, the following (based on Cotton, 2003):

1. Supporting positive school climate is one of the most fundamentally important goals. Cotton (2003) explains, "Almost everything that the principal says and does contributes to the overall school climate" (p. 69).

2. Paying attention to rituals, ceremonies, and other symbolic actions strengthens "a sense of affiliation with the school" (Cotton, 2003, p. 69). Effective principals realize that school culture honors tradition; instills school pride; and recognizes the achievements and contributions of teachers, students, and parents.

3. Establishing a commitment to shared vision and goals is critical. Visionary leadership that emphasizes "academic goals of the school and the importance of learning" (Cotton, 2003, p. 68) is essential.

4. Communicating and maintaining high expectations for student achievement is a chief concern of a cultural leader. Cultural leaders believe that all students can learn and that all teachers can succeed. The principal affirms the potential of all students and teachers.

5. Communicating and interacting with the school community on a continuous basis is important in order to build positive relationships. Such relationships positively affect culture and climate.

6. Supporting risk taking among teachers improves student learning. Good principals encourage teachers to experiment and innovate.

7. Maintaining high visibility and accessibility is good for school climate.

Reproducible #6. Communication Techniques

Listening	Nonverbal cues	Reflecting and clarifying
"Uh-huh."	Affirmative nods and smiles	"You're angry because . . ."
"OK."	Open body language (e.g., arms open)	"You feel . . . because . . ."
"I'm following you."	Appropriate distance from speaker—not too close or too far	"You seem quite upset."
"For instance?"	Eye contact	"So, you would like . . ."
"And?"	Nondistracting environment	"I understand that you see the problem as . . ."
"Mmm."	Face speaker and lean forward	"I'm not sure, but I think you mean . . ."
"I understand."	Barrier-free space (e.g., desk not used as blocker)	"I think you're saying . . ."
"This is great information for me."		
"Really?"		
"Then?"		
"So?"		
"Tell me more."		
"Go on."		
"I see."		
"Right."		

Reproducible #7. Barriers to Communication

Barrier type	Examples
1. Judging	1. Judging
• Criticizing	• "You are lazy; your lesson plan is poor."
• Name calling and labeling	• "You are inexperienced, an intellectual."
• Diagnosing—analyzing motives instead of listening	• "You're taking out your anger on her."
• Praising evaluatively	"You're terrific!"
2. Solutions	2. Solutions
• Ordering	• "You must . . ." "You have to . . ." "You will . . ."
• Threatening	• "If you don't . . ." "You had better or else."
• Moralizing or preaching	• "It is your duty/responsibility; you should . . ."
• Inappropriate questioning or prying	• "Why?" "What?" "How?" "When?"
• Advising	• "What I would do is . . ." "It would be best for you to . . ."
• Lecturing	"Here is why you are wrong . . ." "Do you realize . . . ?"
3. Avoiding the other's concerns	3. Avoiding the other's concerns
• Diverting	• "Speaking of . . ." "Apropos . . ." "You know what happened to . . . ?"
• Reassuring	• "It's not so bad . . ." "You're lucky . . ." "You'll feel better."
• Withdrawing	• "I'm very busy . . ." "I can't talk right now . . ." "I'll get back to you . . ."
• Sarcasm	• "I really feel sorry for you."

Reproducible #8. Comparison of Old and New Paradigms of the Six Domains

Domains	Old paradigm	New paradigm
Teaching and learning	• Teaching is simple. • Principals are experts. • Knowledge is transferred to students.	• Teaching is complex. • Principals are facilitators. • Knowledge is constructed by learners from experience.
Collegiality	Impersonal/bureaucratic relationships prevail.	Personal relationships are fostered within a learning community.
Context expertise	Principals work in isolation of others.	Principals create multiple connections in which diversity is appreciated and fostered.
Continuous learning	Focus is on the improvement of learner.	Focus is on the growth of the principal as well.
Change process	Things are fixed, predictable, and unambiguous.	Things are complex, unpredictable, and ambiguous (chaos theory).
Moral purpose	Individual feels disempowered. Individual is subservient to organization.	Self-efficacy is affirmed and individuality valued.

Reproducible #9. Realities of Cultural Leadership: In-Basket Simulations

During an interview you are asked to respond to the following scenarios:

• The previous principal was removed for what the superintendent called "incompetence." Yet, the majority of the school faculty "loved" the principal because he was "easygoing" and infrequently observed teachers. You are the newly assigned principal to this school, in which reading and math standardized test scores have dropped precipitously over the past three years. Many of the teachers have worked in a culture that gave them almost carte blanche over instructional, curricular, and other school decisions. What are your short- and long-term goals, and how do you intend to reverse the climate that prevails?

• The former principal was a bureaucrat par excellence. You believe, in contrast, in building collaborative partnerships that encourage shared decision making. What will be your greatest challenges and what steps would you take to introduce participatory school management?

• How would you forge a role for yourself as a cultural leader and not merely a manager or technician?

• Name the concrete and specific steps you would take to achieve each of the following:
    1. Building stronger, more trusting relationships with students
    2. Building trusting relationships with teachers
    3. Nurturing an ethic of caring schoolwide
    4. Building staff morale
    5. Actualizing your vision for the school
    6. Leading in culturally relevant ways
    7. Resolving conflicts between two faculty members

• Your vision to institute schoolwide inclusion is being met with much resistance by many teachers and parents. Yet you remain committed to inclusion. What immediate steps could you take to move your vision forward? How will you deal with teacher and parent resistance? One parent adamantly proclaims, "Under no circumstances will I allow my child in a class with 'them.'"

• You are a principal in an ethnically diverse school. All the African American students sit by themselves in the cafeteria. What's your reaction? What would you do, if anything, to foster intergroup interaction, respect, and cooperation?

• A teacher in your school chastises a student for not looking at her in the "eyes" when posing a question. The matter comes to your attention. What would you do or say?

• A new balanced literacy program is mandated by the district. Teachers refuse to change the way they have been teaching. How do you introduce the new approach without ostracizing the teachers or ignoring their feelings?

• The chairperson of the math department has a verbal dispute with one of the school's senior teachers. The teacher then resigns, as do three other teachers in the department, leaving the department half-staffed. The four teachers, unbeknownst to you, all secure positions in another district. How do you deal with the conflict that ensues, and what do you do or say to the chairperson?

• You respond to an ad that reads, in part, "Principal wanted: A strategic thinker, leader, and manager who will embrace a clear vision of the Wayne Brook Elementary School's future that distinguishes its programs and services from other schools in the region.... A strong commitment to working in a diverse and multicultural community is essential." What would you say during the interview to demonstrate that you are the person for the position?

Reproducible #10. Assessing Your Role as Cultural Leader

SA = Strongly Agree ("For the most part, yes.")
A = Agree ("Yes, but . . .")
D = Disagree ("No, but . . .")
SD = Strongly Disagree ("For the most part, no.")

SA A D SD 1. Teachers willingly volunteer to serve on school-based decision-making teams and other grade or schoolwide committees.

SA A D SD 2. Teachers display enthusiasm and commitment to school goals and objectives.

SA A D SD 3. A feeling of togetherness pervades the grade or school.

SA A D SD 4. School governance is characterized by teachers as democratic participants.

SA A D SD 5. Teachers are encouraged by the principal to get involved in decision making.

SA A D SD 6. Teachers are aware of the school's mission and goals.

SA A D SD 7. A problem-solving ethos pervades the school.

SA A D SD 8. The principal takes the lead in setting a positive tone (i.e., friendliness and supportive environment).

SA A D SD 9. Teachers fear change.

SA A D SD 10. Teachers and principal work as a learning team.

SA A D SD 11. Teachers feel threatened by the principal's presence.

SA A D SD 12. Teachers are suspicious of the principal's motives.

SA A D SD 13. Parents are not welcome in the school building.

SA A D SD 14. Teachers encourage parental involvement by word and deed.

SA A D SD 15. A pessimistic atmosphere pervades the school.

SA A D SD 16. The principal is upbeat and positive (i.e., sees the glass as half full).

SA A D SD 17. Teachers articulate that they are proud of their accomplishments.

SA A D SD 18. Teachers' opinions are solicited and are used to shape school policy.

SA A D SD 19. Policies and procedures related to teachers are fair and equitable.

SA A D SD 20. Policies and procedures related to students are fair and equitable.

SA A D SD 21. Policies and procedures related to parents are fair and equitable.

SA   A   D   SD   22. Lines of communication between parents and teachers are open.

SA   A   D   SD   23. Innovative teaching practices are encouraged.

SA   A   D   SD   24. When problems emerge, established procedures are in place to address them.

SA   A   D   SD   25. The principal encourages risk raking and change.

SA   A   D   SD   26. Parents are welcome in the classroom, at appropriate times.

SA   A   D   SD   27. Parents are aware of the school's goals.

SA   A   D   SD   28. Students are aware of the school's goals.

SA   A   D   SD   29. Teachers enjoy getting together informally.

SA   A   D   SD   30. Faculty takes pride in each other's accomplishments.

SA   A   D   SD   31. The principal is insecure and uncertain about how to plan for the future.

SA   A   D   SD   32. Teachers trust the principal.

SA   A   D   SD   33. Students trust the principal.

SA   A   D   SD   34. Parents trust the principal.

SA   A   D   SD   35. The principal is accessible to parents.

SA   A   D   SD   36. The principal is accessible to teachers.

SA   A   D   SD   37. The principal is accessible to students.

SA   A   D   SD   38. The principal tries to cover up problems.

SA   A   D   SD   39. The principal solicits and values the opinions of others.

SA   A   D   SD   40. Workshops are planned collaboratively.

SA   A   D   SD   41. Teachers' opinions are solicited and used to improve the school in some way.

SA   A   D   SD   42. Student misbehavior goes unpunished.

SA   A   D   SD   43. The principal is generally well liked by teachers.

SA   A   D   SD   44. The principal is pleasant, cooperative, and supportive of teachers.

SA   A   D   SD   45. The principal is a strong advocate of student rights.

SA   A   D   SD   46. Rules and regulations are applied fairly and judiciously.

SA   A   D   SD   47. Most parents support school policies.

SA   A   D   SD   48. The school has an outstanding reputation in the community.

SA   A   D   SD   49. The principal cares for teachers' feelings.

SA   A   D   SD   50. The principal supports teachers in student disciplinary matters.

SA   A   D   SD   51. Students enjoy coming to school.

SA   A   D   SD   52. Teachers enjoy coming to school.

SA   A   D   SD   53. The principal rewards teachers for going beyond the call of duty.

SA   A   D   SD   54. The principal is blatantly prejudiced.

SA   A   D   SD   55. Innovations are encouraged.

SA   A   D   SD   56. Students are involved in decision making.

SA   A   D   SD   57. Students report that they have a feeling of belonging to the school community.

SA   A   D   SD   58. Students keep their classrooms, corridor, and school building clean (e.g., clean of graffiti).

SA   A   D   SD   59. The principal, by word and deed, supports cultural diversity.

SA   A   D   SD   60. The principal maintains high expectations for performance and emphasizes instructional excellence.

Part III

Book Three:
What Every Principal Should Know About Ethical and Spiritual Leadership

**Overview of Ethical and Spiritual Leadership:
Flex Some Moral Muscle to Strengthen Lifelong
Learning and Achievement**

Values-based leadership has an exponential impact—from the classroom and campus to the community and beyond. By championing solid instruction in ethical problem solving and embodying moral ideals, principals can make a meaningful difference in students' current and future success.

This third volume of a seven-part leadership series offers practical strategies infused with passionate insights about principals' vital role as ethical and spiritual leaders. Research based and inspirational, *What Every Principal Should Know About Ethical and Spiritual Leadership* equips new and veteran administrators with the tools and reflective prompts needed to become esteemed role models. Included within are best practices for upholding the spiritual, ethical, and moral dimensions of leadership; five essential virtues for leading with conviction; and tactics for resolving real-world ethical dilemmas.

By focusing on these often-overlooked aspects of leadership, the author provides an invaluable sounding board for principals to shape their own beliefs-driven decisions and actions. Key concepts are readily accessible through such features as:

- "Before We Get Started" questionnaire and response analysis (TAKE THE SURVEY NOW on pages xiii–xv.)
- Case study and accompanying reflective questions (READ THE CASE STUDY NOW and answer the reflective questions on pages 14–16.)

- "What You Should Know About" section framing each chapter
- Self-assessment resource for determining strengths in ethical and spiritual leadership

Best Practices in Leading Ethically, With Moral Purpose, and With an Awareness of the Spiritual

Overview

This chapter encourages principals to lead ethically, with moral purpose, and with an awareness of the spiritual. Although educators may have shared meaning regarding ethical and moral behavior, they are likely less clear on the spiritual. Still, this chapter attempts to provide some concrete examples and explanations of the spiritual part of a principal's responsibility. Effective principals as ethical and spiritual leaders should know something about both of these areas that have an impact on teaching and on their relationships with others:

- **Maintaining Assumptions About Ethics**—We review some ideas about ethical and moral principles by Zubay and Soltis (2005).
- **Creating and Sustaining an Ethical Organization**—We review Nash's (1990) four qualities for doing so.
- **Affirming Three Qualities for a Moral Life**—We review Starratt's (1996) three qualities for doing so.
- **Following Seven Spiritual Gateways**—We review Kessler's (2000) seven gateways for enhancing the spiritual.
- **Becoming a Holistic Educator**—We review Gallegos Nava's (2001) ideas for becoming holistic.

Discussion Questions

1. What is the difference between the ethical and the moral?

2. How would you define the "spiritual" part of a principal's job?

3. What is the relationship among ethics, morality, and spirit?

4. What types of ethical situations or dilemmas might a principal confront in the course of a given week?

5. Can someone be taught to behave ethically?

6. What "moral imperatives" guide your actions as principal?

7. Can educators agree on a common set of moral values? Explain.

8. How can a principal create and sustain an ethical organization?

9. Is it possible to serve as a principal without a sense of one's spirituality? Explain.

10. What does holistic education mean to you?

11. How would you characterize your personal sense of ethics?

12. Can someone behave unethically or immorally in one's personal life but still serve admirably as principal?

Engagement Activity

Time: 40 minutes

Materials: chart paper, markers, masking tape, *What Every Principal Should Know About Ethical and Spiritual Leadership* by Jeffrey Glanz

Divide the group into three smaller groups. Post a piece of chart paper on a wall near where each group is meeting. Have group members assign a recorder. After 20 minutes of group work, reconvene and have each group report out.

Group 1: The Ethical

Define "ethical" behavior or a sense of "ethics" in the principalship. Brainstorm five different situations or circumstances that one might categorize as ethical dilemmas. Draw from real-life experiences, personal or otherwise. Brainstorm possible ways to address the dilemma.

Group 2: The Moral

Define "moral" behavior or a sense of "morality" in the principalship. Brainstorm five moral choices a principal might make and five behaviors that one might categorize as immoral. Draw from real-life experiences, personal or otherwise. Brainstorm possible ways to address these moral choices and circumvent these immoral acts.

Group 3: The Spiritual

After reading portions of the chapter, define spirituality. Brainstorm examples that might demonstrate the spiritual side of a principal's work. What ways can you suggest to raise the consciousness of principals who do not appreciate or recognize the spiritual?

As a follow-up activity, take the surveys at the end of the chapter, pages 27–34. What did you learn about yourself?

Best Practices for Leading With Soul and Conviction

Overview

This chapter addresses the imperative for leaders to lead with soul and conviction. Following Bolman and Deal's (1997) lead, *soul* is defined as a bedrock sense of what principals believe in, what they care about, and who they really are as individuals. A leader with a sense of *soul* possesses a well-defined value system and a deep sense of self (Hoyle, 2002). Soulful leaders are aware of their unique qualities that make them particularly effective as leaders. Conversely, they are also aware of their limitations. Moreover, following Hare's (1993) lead, principals must also possess essential characteristics, "virtues" (according to Hare) or, as is referred to in this chapter, "excellences." This chapter focuses on the influence of the individual, personifying virtues and excellences, as most critical in terms of successful leadership. Effective principals as ethical and spiritual leaders should know how to lead with soul and conviction. They should exhibit:

- **Courage**—Principals remain steadfast in their beliefs and thus exhibit moral fortitude.
- **Impartiality**—Principals commit to maintain a nonpartisan, unbiased position.
- **Empathy**—Principals identify with and feel another's pain.

> • **Good judgment**—Principals are good decision makers because they weigh evidence fairly.
> • **Humility**—Principals are aware of their limitations but at the same time are cognizant of their abilities.

Discussion Questions

1. What is the relationship between ethics/spirituality and soul/conviction?

2. Is it possible to behave unethically yet with conviction? Explain.

3. Is it possible to act immorally but still lead with soul? Explain.

4. Can one develop certain virtues or excellences, or are they innate?

5. Who are the kinds of principals that we should attract to the position?

6. What does leading with soul look like? Provide concrete examples.

7. What does leading with conviction look like? Provide concrete examples.

8. How have you acted courageously? Provide one specific instance.

9. Are you always impartial? Is it possible to be so? Explain.

10. Must all principals demonstrate empathy? Explain.

11. Describe a case in which you did not judge ethically. What were the consequences of your decision?

12. How is it possible for a principal to remain humble but at the same time lead a school?

Engagement Activity

Time: 40 minutes

Materials: *What Every Principal Should Know About Ethical and Spiritual Leadership* by Jeffrey Glanz

Refer to the "What You Should Know About Leading With Soul and Conviction" section on pages 37–51. Divide the group into five smaller groups. Provide each member of each group with one of the five subsections of the chapter:

• Exhibiting Courage
• Maintaining Impartiality
• Demonstrating Empathy
• Judging Ethically
• Remaining Humble

Instruct each member to read the subsection and be prepared to react to the contents by answering:

1. What did you agree with?

2. What did you disagree with?

3. How did you react to the suggestions offered?

Have participants then discuss among themselves the Reflective Question at the end of each subsection. Assign a member or two to report out to the whole group.

After 25 minutes of group work, reconvene and have each group report out. Discuss what it means to lead with soul and conviction. Does the group have a firmer understanding of soul and conviction?

As a follow-up activity, challenge members to identify individuals during the course of the next week who may or may not have acted courageously, with impartiality, with good judgment, who may or may not have judged ethically, and who may or may not have acted humble.

Best Practices for Resolving Ethical Dilemmas

Overview

Principals often encounter intractable ethical dilemmas. How do they respond to these challenges? What are the skills or experiences they might draw upon to deal with such difficulties? This chapter highlights three approaches for resolving ethical dilemmas:

- **The Rest Model**—Principals should exhibit moral sensitivity, moral judgment, moral motivation, and moral action when working through an ethical dilemma.
- **Five Principles of Ethics**—Principals must respect autonomy, do no harm, benefit others, be just, and be faithful when undertaking ethical decision making.
- **Twelve Questions**—Principals should pose 12 questions before making any ethical decision.

Discussion Questions

1. What are some of the ethical dilemmas a principal may face on a daily basis?

2. How have you seen other principals confront such dilemmas? What strategies did they use successfully? Unsuccessfully?

3. What does it mean to say that confronting an ethical issue requires a sound moral grounding?

4. What strategies have you used as principal that have been successful?

Engagement Activity

Time: 40 minutes

Materials: *What Every Principal Should Know About Ethical and Spiritual Leadership* by Jeffrey Glanz

Refer to the "What You Should Know About Approaches to Resolving Ethical Dilemmas" section on pages 55–61. Divide the group into three smaller groups. Have group members assign a recorder. Let each group identify a major, troubling ethical dilemma that a principal might encounter. Have each group apply each of the three approaches discussed in the chapter. Which model or approach was most helpful in addressing the dilemma? After 20 minutes of group work, reconvene and have each group report out.

Culminating Activity

Time: 60–90 minutes

Materials: This culminating activity utilizes Resources A and B in *What Every Principal Should Know About Ethical and Spiritual Leadership* by Jeffrey Glanz.

Divide the participants into two groups. One group will work on Resource A and the other group will work on Resource B. Make sure to provide copies of each Resource to each group (only one for each group, not one copy for each group member because the group participation of all members will be enhanced by giving only one copy for the group). Allow groups to assign responsibilities to members:

Recorder—person responsible for recording info for group

Monitor—ensures that each group member participates (e.g., in the case of a silent member, the monitor might ask, "Steve, what do you think?" or "Do we all agree on the solution?")

Captain—ensures group stays on task to complete assigned task

Reporter—reports out to large group at end of session (may be one or two individuals)

What other roles/responsibilities can you encourage?

Resource A
   Select as many in-basket simulations as time permits and brainstorm three specific strategies for coping/dealing with each scenario. Ensure all group members agree on each strategy (prioritize them here as relevant). During the report out phase, rather than just reading the scenario and reporting strategies, the group should first encourage audience reaction and participation and only then share group strategies.

Resource B
   Members administer the survey to the entire group. In other words, all session participants take the survey anonymously. Group members then tabulate results for later presentation and discussion. Afterwards, Resource B group members offer their personal insights to questionnaire items. For instance, someone might share that she doesn't really feel comfortable giving workshops to teachers in a particular area. Discussion should occur within a collegial, non-threatening, but supportive environment encouraging alternate ways of seeing things and offering positive, constructive suggestions. During the reporting out session, group members should plan, in advance, key questions to provoke audience participation.

Ethical and Spiritual Leadership Reproducibles

Reproducible #1. Questionnaire

Directions: Using the Likert scale below, circle the answer that best represents your on-the-spot belief about each statement.

SA = Strongly Agree ("For the most part, yes.")
A = Agree ("Yes, but . . .")
D = Disagree ("No, but . . .")
SD = Strongly Disagree ("For the most part, no.")

SA   A   D   SD   1. Principals must have an unwavering commitment to ethical standards and conduct.

SA   A   D   SD   2. Ethical standards of performance are subjective in nature; that is, such standards depend on the point of view of the particular principal.

SA   A   D   SD   3. Ethical standards of performance should be assessed solely in terms of prescribed standards from district, state, or association policies.

SA   A   D   SD   4. *Ethics* and *morals* are equivalent terms.

SA   A   D   SD   5. Principals not only must promote academic excellence in terms of higher achievement levels as measured by standardized test scores, but also must work for higher-quality performances on a variety of outcomes.

SA   A   D   SD   6. I am attuned to my spiritual nature.

SA   A   D   SD   7. *Spirit* is too nebulous a term to have much practical use in the work of a principal.

SA   A   D   SD   8. A principal who is ethical by following personal and organizational moral norms is also likely to think and feel spiritually.

SA   A   D   SD   9. I concur with theorists such as Jean Piaget that morals emerge and develop as a result of interacting in a social environment and that genetics play an insignificant factor.

SA   A   D   SD   10. I concur with some theorists such as Jean Piaget that morals are best refined as the individual attempts to resolve personal and social dilemmas in real-life settings.

SA   A   D   SD   11. Societal and cultural beliefs greatly influence one's personal sense of ethics.

SA   A   D   SD   12. I concur with some theorists such as Lawrence Kohlberg that there is no single best way to resolve an ethical dilemma; there are no right answers.

SA   A   D   SD   13. Principals have a moral obligation to be fair, nonjudgmental, and honest in all school and nonschool activities.

SA   A   D   SD   14. Concepts of justice, caring, and democracy are a vital part of the work of a principal, even more so than academic performance.

SA   A   D   SD   15. I am more spiritual than most other principals.

SA   A   D   SD   16. I am more ethical than most other principals.

SA   A   D   SD   17. I believe that principals must demonstrate certain character virtues, such as humility and courage.

SA   A   D   SD   18. Universal moral imperatives of leadership, such as a commitment to democracy and an ethic of caring, are not only possible but necessary.

SA   A   D   SD   19. Resolving moral dilemmas is easier over time and with experience.

SA   A   D   SD   20. Although commonplace, ethical and moral dilemmas are challenging and require deep reflection about one's values and beliefs.

Reproducible #2. Quotations

Examine these quotations on ethics, morality, and spirituality. What do they mean to you?

"Just as physical life cannot exist without the support of the physical environment, so moral life cannot go on without support of a moral environment."
—John Dewey

"Leadership is all about values. Ethics as it relates to leadership is more focused upon the determination of the good toward which the group is working and the selection of proper means for the achievement of that end."
—Spencer J. Maxcy

"'Do we have the will to educate all children?' . . . we continue to struggle to answer it. The question invokes a sense of moral purpose or responsibility. The question carries with it a veiled accusation—that we do not have the will to do so."
—Randall B. Lindsey, Laraine M. Roberts, and
Franklin CampbellJones

"According to Stephen Covey, principle-centered leaders operate in alignment with 'self-evident, self-validating natural laws.' These include such basic principles as fairness, equity, justice, honesty, trust, integrity, and service. These principles point the way for leaders."
—Joyce Kaser, Susan Mundry, Katherine
E. Stiles, and Susan Loucks-Horsley

"Principals must be ethical and aboveboard in every aspect of their lives. All decisions must be based on good judgment and basic moral and ethical standards. . . . This sounds obvious. But some ethical decisions are not so simple."
—Elaine L. Wilmore

"The wise leader models spiritual behavior and lives in harmony with spiritual values."
—John Heider

"Every organization needs to evolve for itself a sense of its own ethical and spiritual core."
—Lee G. Bolman and Terrence E. Deal

"The work of educators differs from that of professionals in other fields in its opportunity to influence the holistic growth of persons and their communities. Teachers and administrators, on a daily basis and over an extended period of time, work with young people as they pass through their formative years. They have the privilege of creating environments where persons can learn and develop as healthy, moral, responsible, competent spouses, parents, workers, citizens, friends, and individuals. This is education. Anything less or different represents a reductionistic, bastardized understanding of our field."
—Lynn G. Beck

"Renewal is about the process of individual and organizational change, about nurturing the spiritual, affective, and intellectual connections in the lives of educators working together to understand and improve their practice."
—Kenneth A. Sirotnik

"I am assuming that to behave ethically is to behave under the guidance of an acceptable and justifiable account of what it means to be moral."
—Nel Noddings

"I use the word soul *. . . to call for attention in schools to the inner life; to the depth and dimension of human experience; to . . . longings for something more than an ordinary, material, and fragmented existence."*

—Rachel Kessler

"We need heroes, people who can inspire us, help shape us morally, spur us on to purposeful action—and from time to time we are called on to be those heroes, leaders for others . . . we seem to need moral leadership especially, but the need for moral inspiration is ever present."

—Robert Coles

"Not everyone in an organization is prepared or willing to do the right thing or has a moral orientation. Some would prefer to take the easy way out, do what is more economical, or take the path of least resistance."

—Susan R. Komives, Nance Lucas, and Timothy R. McMahon

"Being a school leader is not an easy job. In many ways, the moral and ethical decisions are the hardest ones we make. . . . The key is taking time to reflect and genuinely examine our behavior, our goals, our mission—and ourselves."

—Elaine L. Wilmore

"By clarifying personal beliefs about schooling and learning, resolving ethics issues, keeping physically and emotionally fit, reflecting on practice and continuing to grow professionally, the person who is becoming a principal will be able to carry out day to day duties and enjoy life. Nurturing the inner person is not easy, but it is imperative if the principal is to be truly successful and effective in helping the school learning community grow."

—Marsha Speck

"A moral way of being is a moral way of being human. Hence, one's morality will flow from one's humanity."

—Robert J. Starratt

"Even under the best of circumstances, leading in tomorrow's organization won't come easily. It will be a constant struggle resulting in large part from the changing conception of leadership. Each of the previous chapters captures a piece of the struggle and includes ideas for overcoming it. But there is one more piece that we haven't yet looked at. It is the difficulty of wrestling with paradox."

—Jerry L. Patterson

"Ethical thinking and decision making are not just following the rules."
—Kenneth Strike and Jonas F. Soltis

"The soul is where the inner and the outer world meet."

—Novalis

"Some people say that the universe is dead (they call it 'inert'), and that everything that happens is accidental (they say 'random'). Other people, like me, say that the Universe is alive, wise and compassionate. Looking at the universe as dead is one story. Looking at it as alive is another. Which story is true for you?"

—Gary Zukav

"Integrity is a fundamental consistency between one's values, goals, and actions."
—Robert Evans

"Leadership . . . involves opportunities to surface and mediate perceptions, values, beliefs, information, and assumptions through continuing conversations; to inquire about and generate ideas together; to seek to reflect upon and make sense of work in the light of shared beliefs and new information; and to create actions that grow out of these new understandings. Such is the core of leadership."

—Linda Lambert

"As a school leader, your ethical decisions are observed by others within the school— students, teachers, and staff. Your decisions affect these individuals and the school as a whole. The success or failure of the moral space of the school is affected by your moral and ethical leadership."

—Spencer J. Maxcy

"An abundance of caring is a signal quality found in most educators. This propensity to step outside of oneself, to see, hear, and appreciate another human being, increases insight, aids communication, and promotes excellence in instruction. Learners served by caring educators feel more important, demonstrate higher motivation, learn faster and better, and reveal greater confidence about their future. That is education at its best."

—Donald R. Draayer

"Successful leadership and administrative practices depend largely on the principal's ethics. Honesty and ethical behaviors guide the principal's actions and demonstrate the sense of purpose and commitment that a school learning community expects from a principal. Thus, principals must be clear about their core beliefs to be consistent and fair in their daily actions in a school."

—Marsha Speck

"The quest for soul in education can move forward only in communities where educators, parents, and civic leaders are willing to air their deepest differences in a spirit of dialogue and collaboration."

—Rachel Kessler

"For organizations . . . soul is a bedrock sense of who we are, what we care about, and what we believe in."

—Lee G. Bolman and Terrence E. Deal

"I have attempted to go beyond the concepts of leading with heart, soul, and morals and have moved on to the concept of love in an attempt to reteach the lessons of history's great leaders that can renew organizations."

—John R. Hoyle

"The job of the school is to provide students with knowledge and skills and to build character and instill virtue."

—Thomas J. Sergiovanni

"Leading with moral purpose calls for an examination of your assumptions about what is ethical and what is unethical, how far you are willing to go to advance your core values and do the right thing, what you are willing to risk to achieve the values of justice and fairness, and how you will wrestle with an inconsistency between your values and the values of your organization. The goal is not to discover easy answers or quick fixes to these issues but to engage in an ethical analysis and to use your moral imagination in solving problems and dilemmas."

—Susan Komives, Nance Lucas, and Timothy McMahon

"When making decisions involving ethical dilemmas, principals exercise moral authority. . . . Yet . . . few principals have been trained to analyze these types of conflicts because ethical issues have been given little attention in preparation programs for administrators."

—David A. Sousa

"The moral purpose of educators may seem universal, but it has too often emerged as an individual phenomenon—the heroic teacher, principal, or superintendent who succeeds for brief periods against all odds. This moral martyrdom is great for the individual's soul, but it does not lead to sustainable reform. We need, instead, to think of the moral imperative as an organizational or systemic quality."

—Michael Fullan, Al Bertani, and Joanne Quinn

"In a high-stakes context, school leaders must search for ways to create a culture of high expectations and support for all students and a set of norms around teacher growth that enables teachers to teach all students well."

—Linda Lambert

"It is time we had a new kind of accountability in education—one that gets back to the moral basics of caring, serving, empowering and learning."

—Michael Fullan and Andy Hargreaves

"The essential value of the public school in a democracy . . . [is] to ensure an educated citizenry capable of participating in all discussions, debates, and decisions to further the wellness of the larger community and protect the individual right to 'life, liberty, and the pursuit of happiness.'"

—Carl D. Glickman

"Democratic schools in postmodern times require stronger leadership than traditional, top down, autocratic institutions. The nature of that leadership, however, is markedly different, replacing the need to control with the desire to support. Ironically, such leaders exercise much more influence where it counts, creating dynamic relationships between teachers and students in the classroom and resulting in high standards of academic achievement."

—Eric Nadelstern, Janet R. Price, and Aaron Listhaus

Reproducible #3. Eight Assumptions of Ethical Leadership

This work is also guided by eight assumptions of ethical leadership reviewed by Komives and colleagues (1998), citing Lucas and Anello (1995):

1. Ethics is the heart of leadership—leading with integrity.

2. All leadership is value driven—treating others justly and fairly.

3. The journey to ethical leadership begins with an examination of personal values—reflecting on one's core values. These values serve as moral compasses to guide decisions you make about ethical dilemmas you face.

4. Ethical leadership can be learned in a variety of ways—through personal experience, trial and error, reflection, and so on.

5. Ethical leadership involves a connection between ethical thought and action—what is necessary is not to learn many ethical theories and philosophical works, but rather to engage in reflecting personal values applied to real ethical dilemmas.

6. Character development is an essential ingredient of ethical leadership—"walking the talk."

7. Members at all levels of an organization or community have the opportunity and responsibility to participate in the process of exercising ethical leadership—all members of the school have responsibility to act ethically and to advance core values of the school.

8. Everything we do teaches—we are role models, and our actions speak louder than our words.

Reproducible #4. Survey to Assess Selected Ethical/Spiritual Dispositions

Respond #1

SA = Strongly Agree ("For the most part, yes.")
A = Agree ("Yes, but . . .")
D = Disagree ("No, but . . .")
SD = Strongly Disagree ("For the most part, no.")

SA	A	D	SD	1. I get asked for help a lot, and I have a hard time saying no.
SA	A	D	SD	2. When I meet a person, I'll give that individual the benefit of the doubt; in other words, I'll like the person until he or she gives me a reason not to.
SA	A	D	SD	3. People usually like me.
SA	A	D	SD	4. I'm happiest interacting with people and aiding them in some way.
SA	A	D	SD	5. People tell me I have a great sense of humor.
SA	A	D	SD	6. I'm good at smoothing over others' conflicts and helping to mediate them.
SA	A	D	SD	7. I believe that respect for authority is one of the cornerstones of good character.
SA	A	D	SD	8. I feel I'm good at supervising a small group of people, and I enjoy doing so.
SA	A	D	SD	9. I want my life to mean something.
SA	A	D	SD	10. I am more spiritual than most of my friends.

Note that the items (previous and following) are drawn from one of my previous books, *Finding Your Leadership Style: A Guide for Educators*, published by the Association for Supervision and Curriculum Development (Glanz, 2002). For a more detailed analysis, please refer to that work.

Respond #2

SA = Strongly Agree ("For the most part, yes.")
A = Agree ("Yes, but . . .")
D = Disagree ("No, but . . .")
SD = Strongly Disagree ("For the most part, no.")

SA	A	D	SD	1. I acknowledge another point of view when data indicate that the other's position is more accurate.
SA	A	D	SD	2. When I make up my mind about an important educational issue or matter, I easily alter my stance if presented with information contrary to my stance.
SA	A	D	SD	3. In making decisions, I can absorb varied positions and pieces of evidence, and I usually remain neutral before I render my final decision, even in cases in which I may have vested interests.

SA   A   D   SD   4. Despite natural inclinations, I would not favor someone from my own ethnic group in rendering a decision about an educational matter.

SA   A   D   SD   5. I am not stubbornly close-minded when I know I am right.

SA   A   D   SD   6. I do not consciously make prejudgments about people.

SA   A   D   SD   7. I am usually consulted because people consider me fair and nonjudgmental.

SA   A   D   SD   8. I value honesty in words and action, and I have an unwavering commitment to ethical conduct.

Respond #3
(Responses are discussed after the questionnaire.)

SA = Strongly Agree ("For the most part, yes.")
A = Agree ("Yes, but . . .")
D = Disagree ("No, but . . .")
SD = Strongly Disagree ("For the most part, no.")

SA   A   D   SD   1. When I hear about another's suffering, I am emotionally moved.

SA   A   D   SD   2. I demonstrate my compassion toward others (not part of my immediate family) by truly offering assistance, even going out of my way to do so.

SA   A   D   SD   3. I often think or meditate about the welfare of others and wish them the best of luck.

SA   A   D   SD   4. I would give friends the "shirt off my back" to assist them.

SA   A   D   SD   5. I value commitment to the development of the individual within the school and district, and I value treating all individuals as significant stakeholders in the organization.

SA   A   D   SD   6. Others would characterize me as a person who is kind, caring, nurturing, and sensitive.

SA   A   D   SD   7. I openly give recognition for outstanding professional performance because I sincerely want to acknowledge the contributions of others.

SA   A   D   SD   8. I am responsive and sensitive to the social and economic conditions of students, as well as to their racial, ethnic, and cultural backgrounds.

Reproducible #5. Leadership and Students Achievement

Effective leadership must be intimately connected to promoting student achievement. As identified by Waters, Marzano, and McNulty (2004), research indicates that leadership has been highly correlated with these critical areas of leadership:

- *Culture:* fosters shared beliefs and a sense of community and cooperation
- *Order:* establishes a set of standard operating procedures and routines
- *Discipline:* protects teachers from issues and influences that would detract from their teaching time or focus
- *Resources:* provides teachers with the materials and professional development necessary for the successful execution of their jobs
- *Curriculum, instruction, and assessment:* is directly involved in the design and implementation of curriculum, instruction, and assessment practices
- *Knowledge of curriculum, instruction, and assessment:* is knowledgeable about current practices
- *Focus:* establishes clear goals and keeps these goals at the forefront of the school's attention
- *Visibility:* has high-quality contact and interactions with teachers and students
- *Contingent rewards:* recognizes and rewards individual accomplishments
- *Communication:* establishes strong lines of communication with teachers and students
- *Outreach:* is an advocate and spokesperson for the school to all stakeholders
- *Input:* involves teachers in the design and implementation of important decisions and policies
- *Affirmation:* recognizes and celebrates school accomplishments and acknowledges failures
- *Relationship:* demonstrates empathy with teachers and staff on a personal level
- *Change agent role:* is willing and prepared to actively challenge the status quo
- *Optimizer role:* inspires and leads new and challenging innovations
- *Ideals and beliefs:* communicates and operates from strong ideals and beliefs about schooling
- *Monitoring and evaluation:* monitors the effectiveness of school practices and their impact on student learning
- *Flexibility:* adapts his or her leadership behavior to the needs of the current situation and is comfortable with dissent
- *Situational awareness:* is aware of the details and undercurrents in the running of the school and uses this information to address current and potential problems
- *Intellectual stimulation:* ensures that faculty and staff are aware of the most current theories and practices in education and makes the discussion of these practices integral to the school's culture (Waters et al., 2004, pp. 49–50)

Reproducible #6. Realities of Ethical and Spiritual Leadership: In-Basket Simulations

During an interview, you are asked to respond to the following scenarios:

• You are confronted by an irate parent who claims that a well-respected teacher hit her child after school in the school yard. The parent demands that the teacher be fired and refuses to leave your office until the teacher is brought down to speak with her.

• You receive a call from a teacher 10 minutes before dismissal; she tells you that she intends to frisk all her students and not let them leave because her purse is missing.

• Teachers listen to you talk about the "soul" of teaching. A few teachers approach you afterward to complain that they don't appreciate your raising religious issues during a faculty meeting.

• You see one of your secretaries subtly taking cash from the school lunch jar and placing it in her pocket. You confront her privately, and although she initially denies the accusation, she later admits the offense. She pleads with you to give her a chance and not report or fire her because she's had a stellar two years at the school.

• A teacher breaks the copyright law by distributing Reproducibles to students without gaining permission from the publisher.

• A student is caught plagiarizing and is brought to your office by the teacher. The teacher is vehement in his insistence that the girl be made an example and be expelled from the school.

• A teacher has his 12th-grade students develop a campaign to elect one of the local politicians who is currently running for reelection. The teacher obviously favors the candidate and solicits student help with the campaign after school.

• The influential school board president asks you to hire his nephew for a teaching position, although he may not be the best candidate.

• A teacher reports to you that Maria, a ninth grader, seems "depressed."

• The coach approaches you to let his star football player play in Saturday's game despite a very low grade point average.

• A P.T.A. mom asks you for special preference for her child to enter a special program, even though the child is only minimally competent.

• The superintendent informs you that a teacher called her today to report that you violated a school policy.

• You are committed to social justice. You decide to review teacher applications only from people from underrepresented groups.

• A relative asks you to divulge some private information about a student in your school; in doing so, you'd violate the Buckley Amendment.

• A female teacher confides to you that she has secretly tape-recorded conversations that she has had with your assistant principal; the tapes allegedly demonstrate his sexual harassment of her.

• Someone tells you something in confidence. You agree to listen. The information you hear, however, shocks you. You feel you need to confront the individual mentioned in the communication, because not doing so might negatively affect a committee's work.

• You personally dislike Fred Stevens, a seventh-grade teacher. You can't explain why. Later in the month, you need to send a teacher to a local conference to represent the grade.

You can send Sam Blanchard, but he doesn't have the skills necessary. Fred would be an ideal choice. You hesitate to select Fred because of your feelings toward him.

- Mr. Hal McCullough, principal of Jones Intermediate School, obtains grant money from the district office for the multicultural fair. Although grant regulations indicate that he doesn't have discretion to use the funds for projects other than the fair, he decides to use some money to fund the literacy program.

- You discover that your assistant principal has been making numerous personal calls from the school phone in his office to his brother in California. Fifteen calls per month are documented on the school's phone bills. School policy does not permit teachers to make long-distance phone calls from school phones without express permission from you.

- The custodian reports that noxious fumes from exhaust pipes in the school's storage room have filled the lowest floor of the building, a floor usually unoccupied by anyone but custodial workers. He reports that he has called the Department of Safety, which is sending over two officials to inspect the situation. The custodian tells you he has things under control.

- You're working late one night with no one around. In the serene setting of your office, when the hustle and bustle of the day's activities have waned, you sit back in your chair and take a deep breath. You think about your role as principal and all you want to accomplish. Before you know it, an hour has passed. You slowly rise from your seat with renewed conviction and a plethora of ideas in mind. You can't wait for the next school day to begin. You get to school the next morning and are confronted by the custodian reporting a flood in the basement, a fax from the district office indicating that you are losing your only guidance counselor and an ESL teacher because of budget cuts, and a call from a local reporter requesting your reaction to a story that will run in tomorrow's edition indicating that your school's scores on last year's standardized math test declined by 5%.

Reproducible #7. Assessing Your Role as an Ethical and Spiritual Leader

SA = Strongly Agree ("For the most part, yes.")
A = Agree ("Yes, but . . .")
D = Disagree ("No, but . . .")
SD = Strongly Disagree ("For the most part, no.")

SA   A   D   SD   1. When confronted with a moral dilemma, I avoid addressing the issue, hoping, at times, that it will go away.

SA   A   D   SD   2. Although I may adhere to some formal Code of Ethics, I realize that good decision-making ability is a complex process of matching personal values with contextual factors.

SA   A   D   SD   3. I am deeply moral, and others who work with me would attest to this as well.

SA   A   D   SD   4. Many people are keenly aware that I am a spiritual person.

SA   A   D   SD   5. I intentionally serve as an ethical role model for others.

SA   A   D   SD   6. When confronted with a difficult situation, people know they can rely on me to inspire them or help them resolve the problem or issue.

SA   A   D   SD   7. I am generally contemplative or introspective, and people see me as such.

SA   A   D   SD   8. Most others would say that I try to champion justice and opportunity for all people regardless of race, gender, sexual preference, and so on.

SA   A   D   SD   9. I work very closely with people, because I can easily empathize with their plight or situation.

SA   A   D   SD   10. My superiors would describe me as a person of integrity.

SA   A   D   SD   11. I cheated at one or two times in my professional life, but I acknowledged my mistakes and have tried to strive for improvement.

SA   A   D   SD   12. I have made mistakes that I regret.

SA   A   D   SD   13. I try to do the right things as well as to do things right.

SA   A   D   SD   14. I seek advice from mentors and superiors.

SA   A   D   SD   15. I sometimes spread false rumors.

SA   A   D   SD   16. Others seek my spiritual advice.

SA   A   D   SD   17. I encourage others to achieve their potential.

SA   A   D   SD   18. I often enjoy serene settings where I can view nature and try to relax.

SA   A   D   SD   19. I find it hard to relax.

SA   A   D   SD   20. The ends justify the means.

SA   A   D   SD   21. I spend a great deal of time in reflection, especially examining my past behavior and decisions made.

SA   A   D   SD   22. I often second-guess myself.

SA   A   D   SD   23. I deeply care about those who work for me.

SA   A   D   SD   24. I am not a very good listener.

SA   A   D   SD   25. I'll sometimes say one thing to one person and something else to another.

SA   A   D   SD   26. My prejudices sometimes interfere with my work.

SA   A   D   SD   27. I actively work to combat injustices such as racism.

SA   A   D   SD   28. Others consider me fair and just.

SA   A   D   SD   29. I can sense pain in others.

SA   A   D   SD   30. I "read" people very well.

SA   A   D   SD   31. We have a moral obligation to pay our taxes.

SA   A   D   SD   32. I would not hire an otherwise competent transgendered individual as a teacher in my school.

SA   A   D   SD   33. A group of parents complain about an ad campaign posted by students in favor of gays and lesbians "coming out of the closet." The parents find the ads offensive and demand that you take them down. After some thought, you'd comply with the parents' request.

SA   A   D   SD   34. You need to hire a new social studies teacher. You promise the job to a close friend of a friend. Later, you find a better candidate for the job. You'd make up some excuse to the first candidate in order to hire the better teacher.

SA   A   D   SD   35. I believe in doing whatever brings the greater good to the greatest number.

SA   A   D   SD   36. You are running low on money for the month. You notice that the grocer undercharged you. You'd keep quiet.

SA   A   D   SD   37. You enjoy listening to and relating ethnic jokes.

SA   A   D   SD   38. Almost anyone can justify their actions.

SA   A   D   SD   39. As long as others do not harm me, I don't care what they do.

SA   A   D   SD   40. One of your tenured teachers has recently demonstrated to you that she is burned out. Although a satisfactory teacher in the past, she is now a detriment to her students, academically. You have tried to offer her assistance in many ways, including writing formal letters to her about her behavior. As a tenured teacher, she ignores your attempts to assist her. You know how difficult it is to remove a tenured teacher in your district. You are inundated with so many other matters. Consequently, you'd throw your hands up and give up on the matter.

SA   A   D   SD   41. I often comply with requests when pressured by peers.

SA   A   D   SD   42. I rely on my moral intuition.

SA   A   D   SD   43. A secretary reports that Mr. Smith "eyes" the 11th- and 12th-grade girls. You, too, notice that he's a "looker." Although no student has ever complained about his behavior, you would decide to speak with him about the matter in private.

SA   A   D   SD   44. You would break a school district policy in order to do a favor for a colleague. You know that no one would ever find out, and the matter doesn't involve a very serious issue, although it does involve breaking with stated policy.

SA   A   D   SD   45. I don't get much of a chance for reflection, because my day—and my life—are fraught with challenges and difficulties.

SA   A   D   SD   46. Most other people who work with me would attest that I have a strong sense of right and wrong.

SA   A   D   SD   47. Most other people who work with me would attest that I am committed to social justice.

SA   A   D   SD   48. My work as principal is as much spiritual as it is intellectual and moral.

SA   A   D   SD   49. My personal, cultural values dictate that loyalty to my family supersedes all else. Yet, when my cousin asks for a favor that violates district policy, I have a moral obligation as principal to enforce organizational policies over personal or cultural norms.

SA   A   D   SD   50. Although I am committed to diversity, I would never hire an unqualified African American over a white male.

Part IV

Book Four:
What Every Principal Should Know About School-Community Leadership

Overview of School-Community Leadership: Harness Your Community's Powerful Resources to Support Achievement

Every school exists within the broader context of its community. By tapping into the wealth of resources that abound beyond campus grounds, principals can weave a tightly knit safety net that buoys student learning. If the adage "It takes a village to raise a child" is true, then certainly raising schoolwide achievement is largely dependent on the active involvement of local businesses, organizations, institutions, and parents.

Cultivating strong alliances with community members entails a systematic, goal-centered outreach program—and this comprehensive guide outlines proven, practical strategies for effectively launching, implementing, and sustaining mutually beneficial partnerships. It highlights straightforward best practices for *reaching out to parents,* including specific involvement activities; *building community relationships* that support school initiatives, plus tips for leveraging the media; and *closing the achievement gap* through community resources and reforms.

This fourth volume in a seven-part leadership series features:

- Initial questionnaire and response analysis (TAKE THE SURVEY NOW on pages xiii–xv.)
- Case study with reflective questions (READ THE CASE STUDY NOW and answer the reflective questions on pages 12–14.)
- "What You Should Know About" sections framing each chapter
- Self-assessment resources
- "In-Basket Simulations" exploring real-life examples

Best Practices in Reaching Out to Parents

Overview

This chapter covers eight major ideas that provide a basis from which to generate and maintain meaningful parental involvement in schools. Research confirms that when schools reach out to families and communities, students do better on a range of social and academic indicators (Chavkin, 2000; Haynes & Emmons, 1997; Whitaker & Fiore, 2001). Although principals may "mouth" a commitment to such involvement, sometimes the exigencies of the job preclude ongoing and significant involvement on a wide scale. This book combines research and practical strategies to maximize school-community involvement. Effective principals as school-community leaders should know something about each of these areas:

- **Learning Together**—We review Epstein and Salinas's (2004) "learning together" opportunities in school.
- **Empower Parents**—We review some of Lawrence-Lightfoot's (2003) recent research on parent-teacher relations.
- **Provide Training**—We review an idea once initiated in a school by Lester Kostick, a retired principal in New York.
- **Establish Parent Coordinators**—We review the institution of parent coordinator positions in New York City under the direction of School Chancellor Joel Klein.
- **Foster Parental Success**—We list Thompson's (2004) eight steps to parental success.
- **Publicize Student Presentations**—We discuss Fiore's (2002) suggestion of attracting parents via student presentations.
- **Solicit Parent and Community Involvement**—We look at Marzano's (2003) three research-based action steps to address community involvement.
- **Develop Parent Involvement Activities**—We mention Young's (2004) activities to encourage parent involvement.

Discussion Questions

1. How do you respond to someone who tells you, "Come on, parents just get in our way . . . we're the professional educators"?

2. What are some practical ways you've seen other principals encouraging parental involvement? Have they been successful? How do you know?

3. What are some ineffective approaches to attracting parental interest?

4. A colleague says, "Parents are OK for baking cakes and helping their child do homework . . . that's about it." How would you counter such a statement?

5. How do you handle an irate parent?

6. How do you handle a parent who dominates meetings and is "around all day"?

7. What do you say to a parent who wants a voice in selecting new teachers?

8. What do you say to a parent who wants a major voice in selecting new curricula?

9. Aside from your experiences, can you cite any research that indicates parental involvement makes a difference?

10. React to the practical tips on pages 17–20. Which make the most sense? Least?

Engagement Activity

Time: 40 minutes

Materials: chart paper, markers, masking tape, *What Every Principal Should Know about School-Community Leadership* by Jeffrey Glanz

Refer to the "What You Should Know About Reaching Out to Parents" section on pages 21–35. Ask participants to skim through pages 21–35 to select one subsection. Once they have selected preferred sections, divide them into like groups. Have group members assign a facilitator and recorder. The facilitator leads group members in an open discussion about the value of the suggestions offered in the section while they provide examples from their experience to indicate what has worked particularly well and what has not. A recorder will write down on chart paper all strategies generated by the group that have been successful. After 20 minutes of group work, reconvene and have each group report out.

As a follow-up activity, conduct a role-playing session for each scenario (solicit volunteers to play roles):

- The irate parent
- The complainer
- The dominating parent
- The parent who informs you she simply has "no time"

Best Practices in Building Community Alliances

Overview

This chapter covers nine major ideas that provide a basis from which to generate and maintain meaningful community alliances for schools. Research confirms that principal support for community involvement is essential for a school's success (Sanders & Harvey, 2002). Some principals may say they haven't the time as they are too busy *in* the school building to "get out there" to do the necessary work to build alliances. Research and practical experience teaches us that such an attitude is not in the best interests of students and schools. Principals need to find the time to build community alliances. Not doing so is simply a big mistake. This chapter combines research and practical strategies to maximize community alliances. Effective principals as school-community leaders should know something about each of these areas:

- **Consider Six Types of Involvement**—Epstein and colleagues' (2004) six types of community involvement form the foundation of any community alliance.
- **Form Community Advisory Committees**—Community advisory boards are practical ways of involving a relatively large number of community constituents.
- **Undertake Community Building**—Reynolds (2002) offers several practical tips for building community support.
- **Plan Together**—Gretz's (2003) planning phases for establishing school-community relations are discussed.
- **Develop an After-School Program**—Principals should get involved in developing after-school curricula matched to during-the-day school curricula, as well as

familiarizing themselves with successful after-school programs that have a community focus (Fashola's [2002]) work.

- **Involve Parents and Community**—Young's (2004) tips for engaging the community are highlighted.
- **Avoid Barriers to Implementation**—Three barriers to implementing a community initiative are addressed as well as Sanders's (2001) strategies for overcoming them.
- **Become Media Savvy**—Ubben, Hughes, and Norris's (2004) suggestions for dealing with the media are reviewed.
- **Become Part of a Professional Development School (PDS) Initiative**—Collaborating with a local college or university is a unique opportunity to forge a community alliance that can pay dividends for student achievement.

Discussion Questions

1. What does contructivism have to do with school-community involvement? (Read pages 37–39.)

2. How do you respond to someone who tells you, "Come on, who has the time to get out there . . . I'm not a politician"?

3. What are some practical ways you've seen other principals build effective community alliances? Describe such efforts and results. How do you know they have been successful?

4. What are some ineffective approaches to building community alliances?

5. How do you know that you have built solid community alliances?

6. What resources do you need to better attract community interest in your school?

7. How many hours a month should a principal spend "in the community"?

8. How do you reach out to families? What about to families that are poor, or do you only attract middle- and upper-class parents?

9. In graduate coursework, were strategies for building community alliances discussed in detail? Describe such strategies, if any.

10. Have you attracted grant money to your school? Describe. If not, what would you need to know to do so?

Engagement Activity

Time: 40 minutes

Materials: chart paper, markers, masking tape, *What Every Principal Should Know About School-Community Leadership* by Jeffrey Glanz

Refer to the "What You Should Know About Building Community Alliances" section on pages 39–62. Ask participants to skim through pages 39–62 to select one subsection. Once they have selected preferred sections, divide them into like groups. Have group members assign a facilitator and recorder. The facilitator leads group members in an open discussion about the value of the suggestions offered in the section while they provide examples from their experience to indicate what has worked particularly well and what has not. A recorder will write down on chart paper all strategies generated by the group that have been successful. After 20 minutes of group work, reconvene and have each group report out.

As a follow-up activity, have each member describe a community project that has proven successful. Encourage specificity of descriptions and discussion of the impact such activities have had on school morale, instruction, and on student learning.

Best Practices to Close the Black-White Achievement Gap

Overview

This chapter covers three approaches for dealing with the black-white achievement gap. This subject has been hotly debated and discussed in the media and educational literature. A variety of perspectives and positions prevail. The topic is both controversial and important. Principals can play a pivotal role in addressing inequities between blacks and whites in terms of access to high-quality curricula, instruction, and educational opportunities for learning. Effective principals as school-community leaders should know something about each of these areas:

- **School-Community Clinics**—Richard Rothstein's (2004) astute and comprehensive recommendations for school reform are highlighted here.
- **Early Childhood Education Centers**—Rothstein's recommendations continue.
- **After-School Programs**—Although recommended by Rothstein, after-school programs are discussed with reference to the work of Fashola (2002).

Discussion Questions

1. What does closing the black-white achievement gap have to do with principal leadership in general? In school-community relations in particular?

2. Some would say there is no such gap? How would you respond?

3. How do you respond to someone who says, "We can't do anything, it's all up to the home . . . parents and their community"?

4. How do you respond to a colleague who says, "I treat blacks and whites the same"?

5. What are some practical ways you've seen other principals address this gap in achievement?

6. What can you do as principal?

7. Read the summary of Rothstein's (2004) book on pages 65–67. What is your reaction to his position?

8. What does research say about resolving the gap?

9. How do you translate such research into action?

10. What resources could you secure to help low achievers succeed in your school?

Engagement Activity

Time: 30 minutes

Materials: *What Every Principal Should Know About School-Community Leadership* by Jeffrey Glanz

Convene the group as a whole. Cull key quotations from the book. After reading a quote, engage the group in discussion around these questions:

- What does the quote mean to you?
- Do you agree to disagree with the quotation? Explain.
- How does the quotation help you better understand the black-white achievement gap?
- The quote represents, in some cases, an ideal. How can you make it a reality?

   As a follow-up activity, invite a community official or two (e.g., a politician, a parent) to speak to the group about how communities and school can form strong partnerships. Facilitate a discussion and include an open question-answer session.

Culminating Activity

Time: 60–90 minutes

Materials: This culminating activity utilizes Resources A and B in *What Every Principal Should Know About School-Community Leadership* by Jeffrey Glanz.

Divide the participants into two groups. One group will work on Resource A and the other group will work on Resource B. Make sure to provide copies of each Resource to each group (only one for each group, not one copy for each group member because the group participation of all members will be enhanced by giving only one copy for the group). Allow groups to assign responsibilities to members:

Recorder—person responsible for recording info for group

Monitor—ensures that each group member participates (e.g., in the case of a silent member, the monitor might ask, "Steve, what do you think?" or "Do we all agree on the solution?")

Captain—ensures group stays on task to complete assigned task

Reporter—reports out to large group at end of session (may be one or two individuals)

   What other roles/responsibilities can you encourage?

Resource A
   Select as many in-basket simulations as time permits and brainstorm three specific strategies for coping/dealing with each scenario. Ensure all group members agree on each strategy (prioritize them here as relevant). During the report out phase, rather than just reading the scenario and reporting strategies, the group should first encourage audience reaction and participation and then share group strategies.

Resource B
   Members administer the survey to the entire group. In other words, all session participants take the survey anonymously. Group members then tabulate results for later presentation and discussion. Afterwards, Resource B group members offer their personal insights to questionnaire items. For instance, someone might share that she doesn't really feel comfortable about meeting with community members. Discussion should occur within a collegial, non-threatening, but supportive environment encouraging alternate ways of seeing things and offering positive, constructive suggestions. Group members, during the reporting out session, should plan, in advance, key questions to provoke audience participation.

School-Community Leadership Reproducibles

Reproducible #1. Questionnaire

Directions: Using the Likert scale below, circle the answer that best represents your on-the-spot belief about each statement.

SA = Strongly Agree ("For the most part, yes.")
A = Agree ("Yes, but . . .")
D = Disagree ("No, but . . .")
SD = Strongly Disagree ("For the most part, no.")

SA   A   D   SD   1. Because I am so busy with in-school affairs, I really cannot devote the time to build strong, enduring relations with the community, other than with parents of course.

SA   A   D   SD   2. I think I should devote most, if not all, of my time to working with teachers on promoting good teaching practice in order to promote student achievement. Dealing with non-instructional, community-related issues is simply distracting and would have, in the end, a dubious impact on student learning.

SA   A   D   SD   3. Principals are expected to do it all; we simply cannot. Hold us accountable for those areas we can impact. As for community relations, it's a waste of time.

SA   A   D   SD   4. I acknowledge my responsibility for organizing and implementing an effective school-community relations program.

SA   A   D   SD   5. I sincerely believe that my involvement in building community relations will have a very positive effect on student learning. We cannot simply abrogate our responsibility to doing all we can to promote student achievement.

SA   A   D   SD   6. If we do not actively campaign to forge meaningful school-community relations, our ability to help children succeed academically will be limited.

SA   A   D   SD   7. One of my most important responsibilities is to reach out to parents in meaningful and sustained ways.

SA   A   D   SD   8. I actively seek to engage parents in school governance and decision-making authority in my school.

SA   A   D   SD   9. Building a strong public relations program is essential to my school's success.

SA   A   D   SD   10. I spend a good portion of my week forging community alliances in order to support what we do in school.

SA   A   D   SD   11. I actively campaign for select local politicians because they play an important role in sustaining vital community relations activities.

SA   A   D   SD   12. We educators do not work hard enough to narrow the black-white achievement gap. We can indeed do more and work harder to eliminate such differences in academic achievement.

SA   A   D   SD   13. I play an important role in closing the black-white achievement gap.

SA   A   D   SD   14. Whole school reform necessitates our involvement in and commitment to school-community relations.

SA   A   D   SD   15. I need to do more to build and sustain a sound school-community relations program.

Reproducible #2. Activities of a School-Community Leader

A school-community leader:

- Envisions the school building as nested within a larger community structure.
- Considers ways the school may meet community needs and vice versa.
- Realizes that external community factors may influence student learning even more than what goes on in school.
- Spends much time forging and sustaining relations with parents, certainly, but also with local business people, religious institutions, social and health agencies, and civic groups.
- Thinks creatively about different ways of involving others in school matters.
- Shares information with community partners.
- Listens to community partners about ways of improving the school or suggestions for further collaborations.
- Encourages innovative ideas and thinking by all members of the community.
- Forms committees of internal and external constituents to plan strategically about ways to improve the school, in general, and more specifically, ways of better promoting student achievement.

Reproducible #3. Quotations

Examine these quotations on school-community relations. What do they mean to you?

"The move to community-building in education . . . reflects a growing awareness of the profound need . . . to feel part of something larger than themselves."

—Rachel Kessler

"One of the biggest problems of schools is that they have pulled themselves away from the public. There cannot be a border between the school and the community, where the school ends the community starts."

—Rod Paige

"[Democratic society] must have a type of education which gives individuals a personal interest in social relationships and control, and the habits of mind which secure social change without introducing disorder."

—John Dewey

"The school exists for and serves the community."

—James Scheurich

"Where the importance of parental involvement is explicit in the research, the importance of community involvement is more implicit."

—Robert J. Marzano

"The entire school territory—the community—is involved in the process of education. . . . Communication between parents and other citizens, businesses, health and social care agencies, several levels of government, teachers, administrators, and students is essential and is the glue that binds the learning community."

—Gerald C. Ubben, Larry W. Hughes, and Cynthia J. Norris

"Clearly, more needs to be done to encourage principals to make the most of potential community contributions to student learning. By building partnerships with existing agencies and groups within the community, school leaders can enhance student achievement and success by creating learning communities that have access to resources beyond those within the school."

—Peter Gretz

"Many recent polls conducted by various school administrator associations . . . rated school-community relations as the first or second most important aspect of their job."

—Douglas J. Fiore

"We need to surround kids with adults who know and care for our children, who have opinions and are accustomed to expressing them publicly, and who know how to reach reasonable collective decisions in the face of disagreement. That means increasing local decision making and simultaneously decreasing the size and bureaucratic complexity of schools."

—Deborah Meier

"[We need a] . . . critically imaginative vision that sees leadership as a community effort to redesign schools for the maximization of the interest of that community for the school is not simply an organizational complex, with function and structure, peopled by workers exercising some status or role."

—Spencer Maxcy

"Nothing is more important to our shared future than the well being of children. For the children are at our core—not only as vulnerable beings in need of love and care but as a moral touchstone amidst the complexity and contentiousness of modern life. Just as it takes a village to raise a child, it takes children to raise up a village to become all it should be. The village we build with them in mind will be a better place for us all."

—Hillary Rodham Clinton

"If we really believe family/community involvement is linked to student success, we must stop giving lip service and allocate at least modest sums for staff development, outreach, and coordination of activities."

—Nancy Feyl Chavkin

"In many communities, partnerships involving schools and other community organizations and agencies are addressing . . . challenges. Such partnerships are helping to create community schools that offer supports and opportunities to enable all children and youth to learn and succeed and to help families and communities thrive. These partnerships are enhancing the core mission of schools: improving academic achievement."

—Anonymous (*NASSP Bulletin*)

"Schools [should] develop public relations strategies to inform families, businesses, and the community about family/community involvement policies and programs through newsletters, slide shows, videotapes, local newspapers, and other media. It is critical that the strategies recognize the importance of a community's historical, ethnic, linguistic, and cultural resources."

—Nancy Feyl Chavkin

"By the year 2000, every school will promote partnerships that will increase parental involvement and participation in promoting the social, emotional, and academic growth of children."

—GOALS 2000

"The same sensitivity required for shaping culture internally must be applied to linking the school to parents and other members of the community."

—Terrence E. Deal and Kent D. Peterson

"It is false to claim that higher standards, more testing and accountability, and better school leadership can close the achievement gap. . . . They may be able to narrow it some; by how much remains to be determined."

—Richard Rothstein

"Rather than waste so much time arguing . . . , policy makers, business and community leaders, and educators must learn to work together in new ways to 'reinvent' the American education system so that all students can find both challenge and joy in learning."

—Tony Wagner

"All teachers should be involved in their communities not just because of the obvious reasons but also because of the political ramifications. . . . PR work is needed to demonstrate the many services that a school provides and the good things that occur there."

—John G. Gabriel

"Gone are the 'good old days' when educators were revered and respected for their wisdom and position by parents. . . . Today's parents are a different breed—less trusting of our educational platitudes and quick to point out what they perceive to be stupidity. . . . [Parents] resent being told to 'just trust us.'"

—Elaine K. McEwan

"Research shows that though students benefit modestly from having parents involved at school, what happens at home matters much more."

—Nancy Gibbs

"Research is accumulating that shows that particular parent involvement practices improve student achievement, attitudes, homework, report card grades, and aspirations."
—Joyce L. Epstein and Frances L. Van Voorhis

"School-community partnerships . . . can be defined as the connections between schools and community individuals, organizations, and businesses that are forged to promote students' social, emotional, physical, and intellectual development."

—Mavis G. Sanders

"Each member of the school community stands to benefit from an effective school-community partnership."

—Pete Gretz

"A community-empowered school is one in which all members of the community— administrators, teachers, school staff, students, parents, and members of the local community at large—participate in efforts to achieve a school's goal of improving student performance."
—Mary Ann Burke and Lawrence O. Picus

"When a quality education is denied to children at birth because of their parents' skin color or income, it is not only bad policy, it is immoral."

—Arthur E. Levine

"Those who desire improvements in classroom learning must realize and acknowledge that school reform cannot easily succeed if it ignores the circumstances of their out-of-school lives."
—Richard Rothstein

"A school administrator is an educational leader who promotes the success of all students by collaborating with families and community members, responding to diverse community interests and needs, and mobilizing community resources."
—Interstate School Leaders Licensure
Consortium (ISLLC) Standard

"That there would be personality and childrearing differences, on average, between families in different social classes makes sense when you think about it: If upper-middle-class parents have jobs where they are expected to collaborate with fellow employees, create new solutions to problems, or wonder how to improve their contributions, they are more likely to talk to their children in ways that differ from the ways of lower-class parents whose own jobs simply require them to follow instructions without question. Children who are raised by parents who are professional will, on average, have more inquisitive attitudes toward the material presented by their teachers than will children who are raised by working-class parents. As a result, no matter how competent the teacher, the academic achievement of lower-class children will, on average, almost inevitably be less than that of middle-class children. The probability of this reduced achievement increases as the characteristics of lower-social-class families accumulate."
—Richard Rothstein

Reproducible #4. Suggestions for School-Community Leadership

Some suggestions for making school-community leadership a reality include, among others, the following:

- Examine and clarify your beliefs about your school-community role and ability (efficacy) to make a difference as principal.
- Learn from principals who you know to be school-community leader exemplars.
- Become conversant with the literature and research on school-community relations and leadership.
- Demonstrate your commitment to school-community relations in word and deed.
- Invite a range of community members to participate in meaningful activities, even decisions, about the school.
- Solicit assistance and support from central office personnel and from the superintendent, in particular.
- Take risks to involve others, and seek support from teachers and other school personnel.
- Assess your role as school-community leader; involve others in the assessment process.
- Reach out to specific agencies for assistance by proposing specific projects and ways they can assist your school.
- Don't be shy or reticent; remain assertive, albeit not pushy.
- Offer community partners a built-in incentive for them to participate.
- Devote time and energy to forging and sustaining relationships in the community.

Reproducible #5. Realities of School-Community Leadership: In-Basket Simulations

This section highlights some of the realities of school-community leadership using an approach called "In-Basket Simulations." It is a study technique derived from an approach used when I studied for licensure as a principal in New York City. The approach was developed by the Institute for Research and Professional Development (http://www.nycenet .edu/opm/opm/profservices/rfp1b723.html). Scenarios that you as a principal might encounter are presented for your reaction. For instance, "A letter from an irate parent complaining that her child is intentionally being ignored by the teacher during instruction in class is sent to your attention. What would you do?" Challenging you to confront real-life phenomena under controlled conditions, these simulated in-basket items will prompt critical inquiry.

Here are suggestions to guide you as you complete these in-basket exercises:

1. Think and respond as if you were a principal, not a teacher or an assistant principal.

2. Place yourself mentally in each situation as if the case was actually happening to you.

3. Draw on your experiences and from what you've learned from others. Think of a principal you respect and ask yourself, "What would Principal X have done?"

4. Make distinctions between actions you would personally take and actions you would delegate to others.

5. Utilize resources (personnel or otherwise) to assist you.

6. Think about your response; then share it with a colleague for her or his reaction.

7. Record your response. A day later, re-read the scenario and your response. Would you still have reacted the same way?

During an interview you are asked to respond to the following scenarios:

• You are a newly appointed principal to an intermediate school in which the former principal neither considered community interests nor solicited community members' involvement in any way. You want to encourage school-community relations. What are the first steps you'd take?

• Your superintendent informs you that several parents have registered formal complaints that their views and opinions are ignored at your school. You're asked to explain your parental involvement program as well as to react to these complaints.

• You are principal of a high school in which several for-profit companies want to set up advertisement bulletin boards, of varying sizes. Would you allow such ads if they would increase budget revenues for the school by $40,000 per year?

• A local politician wishes to donate $20,000 in new technologies for your school. Would you accept the offer?

• Two parent groups vie for power in your urban middle school. Elections are weeks away. Each group approaches you for its support. What stance would you take?

• A wealthy alumnus informs you that she wants to donate $500,000 to the school, but stipulates that she wants the money geared for the music education program in your school. You already have a thriving and well-equipped music department and facilities at your suburban high school. You need the money, however, to increase funds for a new literacy-based program that could assist your efforts to increase literacy scores on standardized achievement tests. How would you go about approaching this donor to allow you to use the money with more flexibility? How would you react if she refused, insisting on overseeing how the money would be spent?

• You are a principal of a high school that has experienced enormous demographic changes. The majority of students now come from families considered to be below the poverty line. Demographic changes include lower achievement levels on standardized test scores across the curriculum, lack of parental involvement in the school, and a diminishment of business partnerships with the school. What concrete steps would you take to increase parental involvement and solicit businesses to reinvest in the schools? How would encouraging greater parental involvement and business participation affect student achievement in your school?

• Mr. Smith, principal of Bishops High School in an urban area of a medium-sized city, realizes how important it is to look good to the community. He continually bombards the media (i.e., newspapers, radio, etc.) with ads and information about the school's athletic program. The school's basketball team won the state championship twice in the last three years. Most, if not all, of the school's ads in the community center around athletics. The superintendent calls Mr. Smith into a meeting and congratulates him on such winning efforts and applauds his media savvy. However, he gently suggests to the principal that his future ads should focus on non-athletic school events, and especially, on academic student accomplishments. How would you use the media to bring positive public relations (PR) to your school? Describe your PR campaign in detail, why it's important, and what potential impact it may have on student achievement, if any.

• You are a principal in a midwestern, urban high school in which parents of Mexican descent complain that there is a lack of attention to their cultural traditions as reflected in the school curriculum. The school's population of students of Mexican descent is the third largest, comprising 21% of the student body. How would you approach this situation?

• As principal of a middle school, you have several creative ways to increase parental involvement and attract local business to donate funds to support the new computer lab in the school. Unfortunately, you find little support from your superintendent. In fact, she insists that you, as principal, should be more involved in in-school matters and that you should leave community networking to her. Generally, you and the superintendent do not see eye-to-eye on many matters. In the past, words have been exchanged between the two of you, and no love is lost on most matters. You understand the value of strong community involvement by the principal. How would you work with the superintendent to support your continued efforts in school-community relations?

• Parents complain about a teacher, Mr. Carson, who displays an uninviting demeanor when meeting with parents. One parent complained, "Mr. Carson places all the chairs up on the desk in his room, as if the room is being mopped by the custodian. He speaks to parents while standing up. Consequently, discussions are usually very brief. This is an outrage." How would you confront Mr. Carson about such complaints?

• You find yourself too busy to interact much with the external community. Your primary emphasis during the first three years as principal of an urban elementary school has been to raise reading scores as reflected on standardized tests. After being charged by the superintendent "to get out there," how would you solicit community involvement to directly and indirectly participate to improve student achievement in reading?

• Teachers complain that because children "have so many home problems and parents are not involved," they (the teachers) cannot "help" them. What's your reaction? What actions would you take?

• Parents complain that the after-school program is "just a babysitting service." They demand that you increase the program's academic rigor. How would you react to such complaints?

- Local corporation X turns down your request for a $60,000 grant to support computer technology in your school. What's your next step?

- You've heard from a colleague that some grant money from a state senator's office is available to support your efforts at establishing an after-school tutorial program. What steps would you take to secure the $450,000 grant? Whose assistance would you solicit?

- Parents inform you that they want a more active voice in curricular decision making in your school. Furthermore, they insist on being consulted on all new teacher hires. How would you respond to such demands?

- The superintendent receives complaints from teachers of your suburban elementary school that you pay too much attention to community interests. They say you're more interested in parents' concerns than listening to them. The word about school is that "the principal is a politician, not an educator." One lead teacher in your school complained that you are "a showman, only after the glitz. . . . There's no academic substance to his efforts." He continues, "Sure, the principal brings in these famous actors, politicians, and others, but all he does is showcase our work to them. His only interest is to make himself look good." Admittedly, you do pay an inordinate amount of attention to the community. Yet, you feel that, in the long run, such community outreach can only benefit the school. How would you go about communicating these benefits to teachers and others? How precisely do these efforts affect student achievement?

- During a speech you inadvertently offend some parents for their lack of attendance at school meetings. Your comments spread like wildfire throughout the community. How would you handle this irate call?

> *Parent:* I heard what you said. I do care for my child. I just had
> to work late that night. How dare you imply that I do not care!

- What role would you play in terms of addressing social, political, and/or economic reform in order to promote learning for all students in your school?

Reproducible #6. Assessing Your Role in School-Community Relations

SA = Strongly Agree ("For the most part, yes.")
A = Agree ("Yes, but . . .")
D = Disagree ("No, but . . .")
SD = Strongly Disagree ("For the most part, no.")

SA   A   D   SD   1. I undertake a yearly poll to ascertain parental views on school matters.

SA   A   D   SD   2. I am willing to listen to advice from parents and community members.

SA   A   D   SD   3. I speak to community groups once a month, on average.

SA   A   D   SD   4. I encourage parents to join curriculum committees.

SA   A   D   SD   5. I am politically active in the community by speaking, on occasion, to local politicians and other community members.

SA   A   D   SD   6. I have a school-community relations program firmly established, implemented, and reviewed annually.

SA   A   D   SD   7. I am aware of the average income levels of parents in my school community.

SA   A   D   SD   8. I am fully aware of the ethnic and racial compositions of parents in my community as well as their cultural traditions.

SA   A   D   SD   9. I am in contact with key elected officials in my community.

SA   A   D   SD   10. I know the opinion makers in my community.

SA   A   D   SD   11. I am quite familiar with the geography of the community in which my school is situated.

SA   A   D   SD   12. Within the district in which I work, I visit some sort of community function (outside my school) at least once a month.

SA   A   D   SD   13. I am acutely aware of community health and safety problems and issues within the district in which I work.

SA   A   D   SD   14. I am aware of community recreational and youth programs in my community.

SA   A   D   SD   15. I serve as a member on at least one type of civic organization.

SA   A   D   SD   16. I see my role as fostering communication between my school and the community.

SA   A   D   SD   17. I discuss the importance of school-community relations, along with relaying specific information, to my faculty and staff.

SA   A   D   SD   18. Teachers can assist school-community relations by their own voluntary contacts with the community.

SA   A   D   SD   19. I sometimes invite faculty and staff to partake in community activities.

SA   A   D   SD   20. I invite community representatives to visit my school as often as is relevant and possible.

SA   A   D   SD   21. I am aware of the various alternative educational resources that exist in the community beyond what is offered at my school.

SA   A   D   SD   22. I encourage family and community involvement in decision making.

SA   A   D   SD   23. I believe in professional development schools (PDSs) as a unique opportunity to foster school-community involvement.

SA   A   D   SD   24. My building is usually available for use by community organizations, when approved by district officials and in accordance with local regulations and laws.

SA   A   D   SD   25. My P.T.A. is actively engaged in the community as well as with a variety of in-school functions.

SA   A   D   SD   26. I encourage teachers to take students on field trips to local cultural centers, such as museums and libraries.

SA   A   D   SD   27. I have developed a school-community strategic plan.

SA   A   D   SD   28. Our school has developed a written plan of policies and administrative support for family involvement.

SA   A   D   SD   29. I solicit free educational resources from local businesses and organizations.

SA   A   D   SD   30. I reach out to service clubs that may include Lions, Rotary, Knights of Columbus, and so forth.

SA   A   D   SD   31. I encourage family and community involvement in homework.

SA   A   D   SD   32. I partake in at least one social, civic, or religious association in my own community.

SA   A   D   SD   33. I encourage class reunions, community cultural gatherings, and other varied community-school functions.

SA   A   D   SD   34. I solicit assistance from senior citizens in the community.

SA   A   D   SD   35. I keep faculty and staff aware of community resources, events, and activities.

SA   A   D   SD   36. I solicit business or social agency volunteers to work in my school, as appropriate.

SA   A   D   SD   37. I reach out to religious institutions in my community to find ways of soliciting their assistance with school objectives.

SA   A   D   SD   38. I reach out to the local employers in the school community, including the local grocery stores.

SA   A   D   SD   39. I call on charities such as the American Red Cross and the United Way.

SA   A   D   SD   40. I encourage family and community involvement in fund-raising.

SA   A   D   SD   41. I contact alumni who play a critical role in school-community relations.

SA   A   D   SD   42. I reach out to local colleges to support the professional development of my teachers and others.

SA   A   D   SD   43. I have contacted local hospitals and other health-related agencies to share information.

SA A D SD 44. I keep the community informed in various ways (letters, bulletins, calendars, posters, newspaper ads, etc.) of significant school events (e.g., talent shows, honor ceremonies).

SA A D SD 45. My school has PR (public relations) brochures and materials ready for distribution to the community.

SA A D SD 46. I contact the local radio station to make relevant announcements.

SA A D SD 47. I have invited media to my school to cover a special event or activity.

SA A D SD 48. I know the names and have the phone numbers of key community officials, including the police department, hospital or emergency medical team, radio, newspaper, church, and so on.

SA A D SD 49. I articulate on a regular basis with other elementary, middle, or high schools.

SA A D SD 50. Our school newsletter highlights, in most issues, some aspect of the community (e.g., a civic official).

SA A D SD 51. I undertake fund-raising initiatives in the local community and encourage others to do so, as appropriate.

SA A D SD 52. I continually invite local community officials, including employers and politicians, to my school to discuss ways of furthering partnerships.

SA A D SD 53. I maintain contact with the editor of the local newspaper to advertise school-community events and to solicit assistance for the school in relevant ways.

SA A D SD 54. I discuss with my faculty ways to improve parental involvement and other community involvement in schools.

SA A D SD 55. I undertake an annual evaluation of our school-community relations program.

SA A D SD 56. I solicit feedback from parents, informally and formally, about school-community relations.

SA A D SD 57. My role is to maximize community resources in order to promote student learning in my school.

SA A D SD 58. I am committed to school-community relations and will develop sufficient time to ensure my school's success.

SA A D SD 59. I cannot succeed at school-community relations without the assistance of my teachers.

SA A D SD 60. The most obvious way to ensure a sound school-community relations program is to develop organizational mechanisms that facilitate smooth, ongoing, and productive communications between parents and teachers. Parents must play an active role in school, whenever feasible.

Part V

Book Five:
What Every Principal Should Know About Collaborative Leadership

**Overview of Collaborative Leadership:
Collaborate to Alleviate Stress and Elevate Success**

The demands on today's principals can be overwhelming in their complexity. More than ever, it is critical for principals to engage in meaningful collaboration, empowering staff, parents, community members, and students with a voice in making decisions and making a difference.

By drawing on the collective wisdom of the school's stakeholders, principals can promote a sense of shared conviction and responsibility for heightened levels of success—and this guide will help you get there. It offers a proven three-phased collaborative leadership approach, covering best practices for *team building*—including 10 characteristics of successful teams, the "Twenty-Five Questions" exercise, and team assessments; *action research*—highlighting the three forms of action research, plus steps for implementation; and *shared decision making*—with much emphasis on developing teacher leaders.

This fifth volume of a seven-part leadership series features reader-friendly tools, including:

- Insightful questionnaire and response analysis (TAKE THE SURVEY NOW on pages xiii–xv.)
- Case study with reflective questions (READ THE CASE STUDY NOW and answer the reflective questions on pages 12–15.)
- "What You Should Know About" sections framing each chapter
- Self-assessment resources
- "In-Basket Simulations" exploring real-life examples

Best Practices in Team Building

Overview

This chapter highlights seven characteristics for effective collaborative leadership, 10 characteristics of effective teams, assessment of one's leadership style, an icebreaker activity, an exercise to build and learn together, and finally an evaluative instrument to gauge how well a team is progressing. A major premise is that collaborative leadership requires dutiful attention to team building. After all, how can one collaborate without the prerequisite skills of teaming or learning how to work with others? Effective principals as collaborative leaders should know something about each of these areas:

- **Leading With Passion, Vision Building, and Teamwork**—We review Clifton's seven requirements for effective leadership that impact our work as collaborative leaders, as cited by Bruckner (2004).
- **Ten Characteristics of Successful Teams**—We review Biech's (2001) 10 characteristics of effective teams.
- **Assessing Your Leadership Style**—We review Glanz's (2002) leadership style analysis in order to gain self-knowledge, an important prerequisite to team building and learning.
- **Draw a Pig**—This is an interesting ice-breaking activity useful in team building.
- **The 25 Questions Team-Development Exercise**—An exercise to enhance team members' relationships with one another, to encourage team discussion about work-related topics, and to clarify assumptions about team participation.
- **Team Effectiveness Critique**—Assess how well the team is functioning.

Discussion Questions

1. Why is team building so critical for collaborative leadership?

2. Have you personally ever participated in team-building workshops or activities? Explain.

3. "It's a waste of time," reports a fellow principal. "Teaming is ridiculous, . . . they know who's boss." How would you react or respond?

4. How can team building improve the *learning* of people who participate?

5. What kinds of teams do you have in your school?

6. Examine Beich's 12 advantages of teaming on pages 17–18. How might each advantage benefit your school?

7. Examine Beich's 12 disadvantages of teaming on page 18. How might each disadvantage constrain your role as principal?

8. What do passion, vision building, and teamwork have in common? (See Subsection 1 in the chapter.)

9. Can you list several characteristics of successful teams? (Compare your responses with Subsection 2 in the chapter.)

10. Describe your leadership style in detail. (See Subsection 3 in the chapter.)

11. Why is assessing leadership styles important for team building?

12. Can you describe one ice-breaking technique you've used with a group? Describe its effect. (See Subsection 4 in the chapter.)

13. How might you encourage team members to work well together? (See Subsection 5 in the chapter.)

14. How do you know if a team is working well? (See Subsection 6 in the chapter.)

15. What might be a connection between team building and action research?

Engagement Activity

Time: 60 minutes

Materials: chart paper, markers, masking tape, *What Every Principal Should Know About Collaborative Leadership* by Jeffrey Glanz

Refer to the "What You Should Know About Team Building" section on pages 25–41. Administer the survey on pages 28–33 to the group (15–20 minutes) and follow the directions for interpreting the results. Lead an active discussion. Use the study questions from the following Web site as a guide:
    http://ascd.org/portal/site/ascd
From the home page, click on Publications and then Books, then click on Study Guides for Books and choose Finding Your Leadership Style: A Guide for Educators.

As a follow-up activity, have participants discuss ways they might use the leadership styles survey to assess leadership potentiality in others.

Best Practices in Action Research

Overview

Participating in action research projects goes far toward promoting collaboration in a school. The time spent on such committees deepens personal relationships, strengthens school commitments, and plants the seeds for further collaborations. Action research is an invaluable means to promote collaboration, because the types of activities educators participate in are meaningful rather than superficial, purposeful rather than haphazard, and enduring rather than ephemeral. As principal, you can foster collaboration enormously by encouraging educators and others in your school to work on action research initiatives. This chapter highlights the importance and benefits of action research for collaboration. Four steps of action research are reviewed, along with three popular forms that can be practiced in schools. Two case studies are provided to demonstrate how action research might be practically applied in schools. The chapter ends with a few suggestions for implementation. Effective principals as collaborative leaders should know something about each of these areas:

- **Action Research for Collaboration and More**—Principals utilize action research work to build strong relationships among faculty/administrators and in order to promote student achievement.
- **Benefits of Action Research**—Once we realize the benefits of action research, we may be very willing to implement such work, even though it may be somewhat time-consuming.

- **Steps in Action Research**—Learn the four easy steps that you can apply quite easily.
- **Three Forms of Action Research**—Action research can be used in three ways.
- **Action Research in Action**—Two case studies are provided to show how it works.
- **Guidelines for Implementing Action Research**—Some practical suggestions for principals are offered.

Discussion Questions

1. What comes to mind when you think of the word "research"?
2. What does an "action researcher" do?
3. How does action research differ from traditional research?
4. Have you ever participated in an action research project? Explain in detail.
5. How might action research improve practice?
6. Why is the concept known as "triangulation" so important?
7. How many data-collection techniques can you name?
8. Are some data-collection techniques superior to others? Explain.
9. What is the difference between a survey and a questionnaire?
10. How might you best analyze your data?
11. What is the next important step after you have analyzed data? Explain.
12. What is the best way to most simply report your findings?
13. What else do you need to know to implement an action research project?
14. What does action research have to do with collaborative leadership?
15. How might you employ it to collaborate?

Engagement Activity

Time: 60 minutes

Materials: *What Every Principal Should Know About Collaborative Leadership* by Jeffrey Glanz and PowerPoint presentation on Action Research at http://www.wagner.edu/faculty/jglanz/ppoint

Refer to the "What You Should Know About Action Research" section on pages 52–69. Using the PowerPoint presentation, lead the group through each slide and facilitate as necessary.

As a follow-up activity, show the group a video of a school using schoolwide action research. Visit www.ascd.org for information.

Best Practices in Shared Decision Making

Overview

Collaborative leadership does not occur in a vacuum and is not in the sole purview of a principal. An important prerequisite to meaningful and successful collaboration is empowering teachers by enhancing their own leadership potential within schools. Site-based management is the kind of structure that facilitates or makes possible teacher involvement or collaborative leadership. This chapter covers the following two topics related to shared decision making:

- **Encouraging Teacher Leadership**—Interest in teacher leadership is most directly influenced by the work on shared decision making and is a vital component of collaborative leadership.
- **Site-Based Management**—Meaningful collaboration cannot occur unless a structure is in place for it to occur.

Discussion Questions

1. Why is sharing decision making so critical for collaborative leadership?

2. How do you break away from a leadership mentality based on Boss-Leadership?

3. A colleague says, "How can I share when they don't know what the hell they want?" How would you respond?

4. Do you believe the time spent in such sharing is well spent? Explain.

5. What areas would you not share in terms of decision making?

6. What are some best practices you have witnessed about shared governance?

7. Describe a situation in which shared leadership didn't work. What happened?

8. Describe a situation in which shared leadership worked well. What happened?

9. Under what circumstances might you share decision making and with whom?

10. With whom would you not share decision making?

Engagement Activity

Time: 40 minutes

Materials: chart paper, markers, masking tape, *What Every Principal Should Know About Collaborative Leadership* by Jeffrey Glanz

Refer to the "What You Should Know About Shared Decision Making" section on pages 72–86. Divide the group into two smaller groups. Post a piece of chart paper on a wall near where each group is meeting. Have group members assign a recorder and a facilitator. Have each group work on one of the two subsections of the chapter: teacher leadership and site-based management. Have participants follow the readings and reflective questions. Encourage sharing and reactions. Encourage them to provide specific instances wherein each strategy might be employed in a real school. Discuss shortcomings of each with practical suggestions for resolution. After 25 minutes of group work, reconvene and have each group report out.

As a follow-up activity, lead whole group discussion about shared decision making. What works and what doesn't, and how might such efforts aid in collaborative leadership?

Culminating Activity

Time: 60–90 minutes

Materials: This culminating activity utilizes Resources A, B, C, and D in *What Every Principal Should Know About Collaborative Leadership* by Jeffrey Glanz.

Divide the participants into four groups, each to work with one Resource. Make sure to provide copies of each Resource to each group (only one for each group, not one copy for each group member because the group participation of all members will be enhanced by giving only one copy for the group). Allow groups to assign responsibilities to members:

Recorder—person responsible for recording info for group

Monitor—ensures that each group member participates (e.g., in the case of a silent member, the monitor might ask, "Steve, what do you think?" or "Do we all agree on the solution?")

Captain—ensures group stays on task to complete assigned task

Reporter—reports out to large group at end of session (may be one or two individuals)

What other roles/responsibilities can you encourage?

Resource A
   Select as many in-basket simulations as time permits and brainstorm three specific strategies for coping/dealing with each scenario. Ensure all group members agree on each strategy (prioritize them here as relevant). During the report out phase, rather than just reading the scenario and reporting strategies, the group should first encourage audience reaction and participation and then share group strategies.

Resource B
   Members administer survey to entire group. In other words, all session participants take the survey anonymously. Group members then tabulate results for later presentation and discussion. Afterwards, Resource B group members offer their personal insights to questionnaire items. For instance, someone might share that she doesn't really feel comfortable giving workshops to teachers in a particular area. Discussion should occur within a collegial, non-threatening, but supportive environment encouraging alternate ways of seeing things and offering positive, constructive suggestions. Group members, during the reporting out session, should plan, in advance, key questions to provoke audience participation.

Resource C
   Administer action research test of knowledge and discuss.

Resource D
   Members administer survey to entire group. In other words, all session participants take the survey anonymously. Group members then tabulate results for later presentation and discussion. Afterwards, Resource D group members offer their personal insights to questionnaire items. For instance, someone might share that she doesn't really feel comfortable giving workshops to teachers in a particular area. Discussion should occur within a collegial, non-threatening, but supportive environment encouraging alternate ways of seeing things and offering positive, constructive suggestions. Group members, during the reporting out session, should plan, in advance, key questions to provoke audience participation.

Collaborative Leadership Reproducibles

Reproducible #1. Questionnaire

Directions: Using the Likert scale below, circle the answer that best represents your on-the-spot belief about each statement.

SA = Strongly Agree ("For the most part, yes.")
A   = Agree ("Yes, but . . .")
D   = Disagree ("No, but . . .")
SD = Strongly Disagree ("For the most part, no.")

SA   A   D   SD   1. Principals value collaboration because they realize that the more minds working on a project, the greater the likelihood for its success.

SA   A   D   SD   2. Collaborative decision making should be incorporated whenever a significant decision has to be made.

SA   A   D   SD   3. Most decisions should be made by committee vote and not by the principal alone.

SA   A   D   SD   4. It's possible to fake collaboration.

SA   A   D   SD   5. Democracy demands collaboration.

SA   A   D   SD   6. Collaboration and competition are like oil and water; they don't mix.

SA   A   D   SD   7. Collaborative leadership involves consensus building and diplomacy.

SA   A   D   SD   8. It is possible for administrators and faculty to develop mutual trust and respect for each other as well as to share common beliefs that focus on student learning.

SA   A   D   SD   9. The principal is the key person in a school to encourage a team or school spirit.

SA   A   D   SD   10. Schools can learn much from collaborative enterprises in business.

SA   A   D   SD   11. *Collegiality* and *collaboration* are pretty much synonymous terms.

SA   A   D   SD   12. An effective principal can encourage meaningful collaboration within a relatively short period of time, say, six months.

SA   A   D   SD   13. I have been involved in some team-building activity within the past six months.

SA   A   D   SD   14. I have been involved in some sort of shared decision-making process within the past six months.

SA   A   D   SD   15. I have been involved in some sort of collaborative action research project within the past six months.

Reproducible #2: Collaborative Leader Basics

A collaborative leader, therefore:

- Realizes that schools are too complex for one person to make all the decisions.
- Thinks about different ways of involving others in school policies.
- Shares information with others who have a stake in the particular activity.
- Listens.
- Encourages, trains, and coaches others to participate in schoolwide, subject-specific, or grade-level decision making.
- Forms committees that are empowered to make important curricular and instructional decisions.
- Solicits the advice of teachers and others.
- Reaches out on a daily basis to parents, students, school secretaries, custodians, specialized support staff, and, of course, teachers.
- Believes that collaborative leadership is a moral imperative for a principal in the 21st century.
- Engages the school staff and community in training to help better understand collaborative decision making.

Reproducible #3. Quotations

Examine these quotations on collaboration. What do they mean to you?

"Today's effective principal . . . participates in collaborative practices . . . it is much easier to tell or to manage than it is to perform as a collaborative instructional leader."
—Linda Lambert

"The relationships among adults in schools are the basis, the precondition, the sine qua non that allow, energize, and sustain all other attempts at school improvement. Unless adults talk with one another, observe one another, and help one another, very little will change."
—Roland S. Barth

"The leadership style which had the greatest impact on teacher morale was collaborative."
—Vernadine Thomas

"Collaboration . . . has emerged as the cornerstone for discussions about supervision in education. We believe that the call for collaboration is more than ideological. Learning requires a collaborative effort between student and teacher. In this respect, collaboration can be thought of as the dominant value driving the organization of schooling."
—James E. Barott and Patrick F. Galvin

"It is incumbent upon a principal to serve as a role model for collegiality and foster such relationships among teachers and staff members through a clear focus on student learning."
—Marsha Speck

"The 'collaborative premise' is a belief that 'if you bring the appropriate people together in constructive ways with good information, they will create authentic visions and strategies for addressing the shared concerns of the organization or community.'"
—David D. Chrislip and Carl E. Larson, as cited by Susan R. Komives, Nance Lucas, and Timothy R. McMahon

"The wise leader is he who the people despise. The good leader is he who the people revere. The great leader is he who the people say, 'We did it ourselves.'"
—Lao Tsu

"The old leadership model—in other words, just being a manager—doesn't work. . . . Now school leaders have to know teaching inside and out. They have to know best practices. They have to know how to structure a school to support teaching and learning. They have to know about professional development for ongoing learning—job-embedded, collaborative types of learning."
—Wendy Katz

"The purpose of collaboration is to create a shared vision and joint strategies to address concerns that go beyond the purview of any particular party."
—David D. Chrislip and Carl E. Larson

"A learning organization is an organization in which people at all levels are, collectively, continually enhancing their capacity to create things they really want to create."
—Peter Senge

"Leadership is not something possessed only by a select few people in high positions. We are all involved in the leadership process, and we are all capable of being effective leaders. Through collaboration with others, you can make a difference."
                                    —Susan R. Komives, Nance Lucas, and Timothy R. McMahon

"When we choose co-creation [collaboration], we end separation, the root cause of conflict. . . . They know through responsible participation that they can empower each other and ultimately their institutions and society, thereby creating a life that is meaningful and satisfying for everyone."
                                    —Thomas F. Crum

"It's a mistake to go it alone. By creating alliances even before your initiative becomes public, you can increase the probability that both you and your ideas will succeed. For the next meeting, personally make the advance phone calls, test the waters, refine your approach, and line up supporters. . . . Know their existing alliances and loyalties so you realize how far you are asking them to stretch to collaborate with you."
                                    —Ronald A. Heifetz and Marty Linsky

"Time is a precious resource in schools. Therefore it is essential that collaborative time in schools is focused on capacity building to assure high levels of quality student learning."
                                    —Pam Robbins and Harvey B. Alvy

"Great discoveries and improvements invariably involve the cooperation of many minds. I may be given credit for having blazed the trail but when I look at the subsequent developments I feel the credit is due to others rather than to myself."
                                    —Alexander Graham Bell

"'Networking' [means] 'exchanging information for mutual benefit.' 'Coordinating' [means] 'exchanging information and altering activities for mutual benefit and to achieve a common purpose.' 'Cooperation' [means] 'exchanging information, altering activities, and sharing resources for mutual benefit and a common purpose.' 'Collaboration' [means] 'exchanging information, altering activities, sharing resources, and enhancing the capacity of another for mutual benefit and to achieve a common purpose.'"
                                    —Arthur Himmelman, as quoted by Kathy Gardner Chadwick

"When teachers share in decision-making, they become committed to the decisions that emerge. They buy into the decision; they feel a sense of ownership; therefore, they are more likely to see that decisions are actually implemented."
                                    —C. H. Weiss, J. Cambone, and A. Wyeth

"What distinguishes leadership from other types of relationships is that, when it works well, it enables people to collaborate in the service of shared visions, values, and missions."
                                    —Lee G. Bolman

"Although action research is not a quick fix for all school problems, it represents a process that . . . can focus the brain-power of the entire instructional staff on maximizing learning."
                                    —James E. McLean

"Although team building is a common expression and is well understood, the concept of team learning is relatively new. Traditional team building focuses on improving individual team members' skills as a means for working with each other. It leads to improved communication, contributes to more efficient and effective task performance, and builds stronger relationships among the members. Team learning is different. . . . It is about getting a team to function as a

whole rather than as a collection of individuals. Team learning begins with a high level of self-knowledge and progresses toward developing understanding of and aligning with other team members. It encompasses goals of team building but extends far beyond."

—Joyce Kaser, Susan Mundry, Katherine E. Stiles,
and Susan Loucks-Horsley

"Colleagueship does not mean that you need to agree or share the same views. On the contrary, the real power of seeing each other as colleagues comes into play when there are differences of view. It is easy to feel collegial when everyone agrees. When there are significant disagreements, it is more difficult. But the payoff is also much greater. Choosing to view 'adversaries' as 'colleagues with different views' has the greatest benefits."

—Peter M. Senge

"I believe that a theory of the schoolhouse should strive to transform the school into a center of inquiry—a place where professional knowledge is created in use as teachers learn together, solve problems together, and inquire together."

—Thomas J. Sergiovanni

"When teachers accept common goals for students and therefore complement each other's teaching, and when supervisors work with teachers in a manner consistent with the way teachers are expected to work with students, then—and only then—does the school reach its goals."

—Carl D. Glickman

"Creating a collegial culture within a learning community includes the following interactive and critical elements: mutual respect, conversations about teaching and learning, shared values and vision, clear expectations, time to share, teamwork, professional development, inquiry, and reflective practice."

—Marsha Speck

"Collaborations are the vehicles for those of us who believe we can make a difference."

—Hank Rubin

Reproducible #4. Assessing Your Leadership Style: The Survey

Take the following survey, the purpose of which is to provide feedback to explore your leadership proclivities.

Directions for Completing the Survey

1. Below, you will find 56 statements.

2. Next to each number, write True (T) or False (F) for each statement.

3. If a statement describes the way you think you are, for the most part, then indicate True (T); if the statement does not describe you, indicate False (F). You MUST write True (T) or False (F). Some statements may be difficult to classify, but please indicate just one answer.

4. Your responses are anonymous. The surveys cannot accurately assess these attributes without your forthright responses to the various statements. You need not share your responses with anyone. Obviously, the accuracy of these instruments is dependent both on the truthfulness of your responses and the degree to which you are aware that you possess or lack a certain attribute.

5. Using the chart below, circle numbers that you recorded as true.

6. After you complete the survey by recording your responses in the chart below, follow the directions to tabulate and interpret the results.

Answer Sheet
(True or False to each statement in each survey)

Am I an AAS?	Am I a CAS?	Am I an AS?	Am I a DAS?	Am I a DS?	Am I a DAG?	Am I an AAG?
1	2	3	4	5	6	7
14	13	12	11	10	9	8
16	15	18	17	20	19	21
30	29	22	24	23	28	25
31	39	32	27	26	41	33
35	40	36	37	34	47	42
38	44	46	48	45	49	43
56	55	50	54	51	53	52

The Surveys

1. I feel I'm good at supervising a small group of people, and I enjoy doing so.

2. When I'm in a new situation, such as a new job setting or relationship, I spend a lot of time comparing it to analogous situations I've been in previously.

3. I believe that respect for authority is one of the cornerstones of good character.

4. I enjoy thinking about large issues, such as how society is organized politically.

5. I get asked for help a lot, and I have a hard time saying no.

6. Ever since childhood, I've always seemed to want more out of life than my peers did.

7. When I first enter a new environment, such as a workplace or a school, I make it a point to become acquainted with as many people as possible.

8. I rarely seek quiet.

9. I can work harder than most people, and I enjoy doing so.

10. When I meet a person I'll give that individual the benefit of the doubt; in other words, I'll like someone until he or she gives me a reason not to.

11. The idea of a lifelong and exclusive intimate partner doesn't seem desirable or realistic for me.

12. A lifelong relationship with a romantic partner is one of my goals.

13. I can sometimes work creatively at full throttle for hours on end and not notice the passage of time.

14. I believe that divorce is to be strongly avoided whenever possible.

15. I'll periodically go through extremely low-energy periods during which I have to remind myself that it's only a phase.

16. When it comes to spending and saving habits, I take pride in being more thrifty and less foolish than most people.

17. Being alone does not scare me; in fact, I do some of my best thinking when I'm alone.

18. My extended family is the most important part of my social life.

19. I spend much less time than others do on what I consider pointless leisure pursuits, such as TV and movie watching; novel reading; and card, computer, or board game playing.

20. I procrastinate a lot.

21. My vacations are always highly structured; several days of just sitting in one place and vegetating would drive me crazy.

22. Directing a big job and supervising a lot of subordinates is my idea of a headache.

23. People usually like me.

24. I find myself getting frustrated because most people's worldview is so limited.

25. Networking as a career and life tool is something that comes naturally to me.

26. I'm happiest interacting with people and aiding them in some way.

27. I have a drive to express my ideas and influence the thinking of others.

28. I find myself getting frustrated because most people operate at a slower pace than I do.

29. I find myself getting frustrated because most people are not on my mental wavelength.

30. I generally believe that if individuals behave outside the norms of society, they should be prepared to pay the price.

31. My home is more organized and cleaner than most people's in my neighborhood.

32. Holding one job for decades would be OK with me if the conditions were good and the boss was nice.

33. When tackling a problem or task, my attitude is usually less defeatist than that of others.

34. It sometimes takes an outside force to get me motivated, because I tend to be satisfied with what I have.

35. I enjoy the feeling of my life going along at an even pace like a well-oiled machine; too many stops and starts and ups and downs would really upset me.

36. Trying to lengthen your life by eating the "right" foods doesn't make much sense to me because when your time's up, your time's up.

37. I have no trouble getting people to listen to me and grasp what I'm saying.

38. I understand that detail work is what ultimately gets a job done, and I have the gumption and know-how to tackle details.

39. Working by myself is no problem; in fact, I prefer it.

40. At times, ideas just "come to me," and if I can't put them down then and there—on paper, canvas, and so on—I'll be uncomfortable until I can.

41. I could never be really happy working for someone else.

42. I like associating with influential people and am not intimidated by them.

43. I'm happiest moving and doing, as opposed to sitting and thinking.

44. Throughout my life there's been a pattern of people calling me one or more of the following: "temperamental," "moody," "sad," "flighty," "different," and I never really felt like I was "one of the boys" or girls.

45. People tell me I have a great sense of humor.

46. I believe that blood is thicker than water and that it's more important to be loyal to your relatives than to your friends.

47. I don't have much time or patience for long family gatherings, such as a whole afternoon spent celebrating Thanksgiving.

48. The makeup of my social circle is constantly changing.

49. Managing a big job and having subordinates carry out the detail work is my ideal kind of endeavor.

50. I prefer to work at a job a set number of hours each day and then have the rest of the 24 hours for relaxation.

51. I'm good at smoothing over others' conflicts and helping to mediate them.

52. I thrive on setting goals for myself and then figuring out how to reach them; I can't imagine just drifting through life without a plan.

53. I'm more intelligent than most people, and others almost always recognize this.

54. I can't fathom the idea of holding one job for decades.

55. I find competition distasteful.

56. I would never dress in a flashy, bohemian, or otherwise attention-getting way.

Directions for Tabulating the Results

1. For each category (e.g., "Am I an AAS?") count the number of True (T) responses in that column. Record your fraction score on the chart below. Note that the numerator represents the number of "True" responses and the denominator represents the total number of questions on the survey (which will always equal 8, because each survey has eight questions). For example, if you recorded "T" for seven out of the eight items in the first column, "Am I an AAS," then your fraction will be 7/8.

2. Complete the table below by referring to your responses on the Answer Sheet above.

Am I an AAS?	Am I a CAS?	Am I an AS?	Am I a DAS?	Am I a DS?	Am I a DAG?	Am I an AAG?
T's/8						

Interpreting the Results

1. Your Natural Leadership Quality is found under the category in which you scored the highest number of "True" responses. For example, if you scored 8/8 for "Am I a DS?" then your quality is "DS." Perhaps no category earned an 8/8, but one category (e.g., "Am I a CAS?") had 7/8, whereas all the others were lower (6/8 and less). In that case, your quality is "CAS."

2. Although most respondents will find their highest score in one category, some respondents may have two or more categories with equally high scores. For example, you may have scored an 8/8 in two categories. If so, then your quality is represented by those two categories. If no category received an 8/8, locate the next highest score. For example, your highest score may be 5/8, and three categories may have earned that score. If this is the case, then your quality is represented by those three categories.

3. In the following chart, circle the quality or qualities that scored the highest number of "True" responses.

AAS	CAS	AS	DAS	DS	DAG	AAG

4. The meaning of these results will become clear as you read on. Please note the following caution: No one assessment can accurately assess one's inclinations or abilities. These surveys are meant to stimulate interest, thought, and discussion for purposes of exploring leadership in schools. Examine the results in light of the theories and ideas expressed in this book and make your own determination of their relevance and applicability to you personally and to your work in schools.

SOURCE: From *Who Are You Really?: Understanding Your Life's Energy* by Gary Null. Copyright © 1996. New York: Carroll & Graf, a division of Avalon Publishing Group. Used by permission.

Reproducible #5. Steps in Action Research

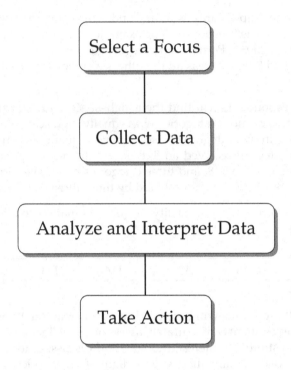

Three Forms of Action Research

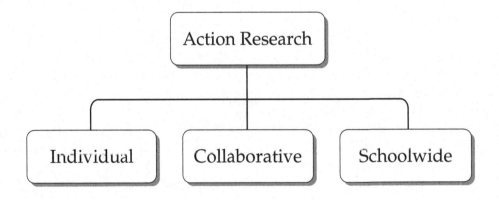

Reproducible #6. Support Site-Based Management, Collaboration, and Shared Decision Making

- *Assess your commitment.* Are you truly interested in bringing others into decision-making processes?
- *Collaborate with others to develop goals.* Have you collaboratively articulated goals and objectives? In other words, what's the purpose for collaborating? To achieve what?
- *Build trust and rapport.* Have you established a conducive, non-threatening environment in which to conduct deliberations?
- *Open lines of communication.* Have you ensured that all interested parties have received notifications or updates via memorandum, e-mail, or otherwise?
- *Set in place conflict-resolution strategies.* Do you anticipate that disagreements may occur? What mechanisms are in place to deal with them?
- *Get involved.* Have you made sure you are highly visible, cordial, and knowledgeable? Have you established the committee and then "disappeared"?
- *Articulate roles, responsibilities, and relationships.* Have respect, clear guidelines, and a chain of command been established and understood by all parties?
- *Keep everyone in the loop.* Are you honest and up front with everyone regarding potential risks and opportunities?
- *Put into place professional development on an ongoing basis, as necessary.* Have you considered the use of professional development activities to assist committee members in communication skills, conflict resolution, consensus building, and so forth?
- *Specify parameters for shared decision making.* Are all parties clear on "who" makes the decisions and how they are made?
- *Provide time and a place for meetings.* Have you established the necessary time and space structures that are so necessary for collaboration to take place?
- *Establish incentives and rewards.* Have you considered the types of positive reinforcement participants want, need, and expect?
- *Identify leadership roles.* Have you considered leadership styles in committee formation and carrying out of responsibilities?
- *Identify opportunities for more collaboration.* What other opportunities for leadership and decision making can you encourage teachers and others to engage in?
- *Always listen.* Do you get out there to listen to complaints as much as you do successes?
- *Form internal alliances.* Are you aware of cliques that may form that may interfere or support a committee or team's work?
- *Form external alliances.* What connections can you make with the community to support internal collaborative work?
- *Keep student learning in mind.* Are you continually aware of why collaboration is so important?

Reproducible #7. Realities of Collaborative Leadership: In-Basket Simulations

During an interview, you are asked to respond to the following scenarios:

• You are a newly appointed principal to an intermediate school in which the former principal was an autocrat. You want to encourage collaboration among teachers, but there's resistance. What are the first steps you'd take?

• Your superintendent informs you that she doesn't like the fact that you're encouraging shared decision making regarding personnel matters. How would you convince the superintendent that such decision making is critical to your role as principal?

• Two members on a school leadership team monopolize committee time with their incessant babbling, often off topic. The team leader is meek and will not confront them. The matter has reached your attention. What would you do, if anything?

• You want to initiate an action research project to address failing writing scores in Grade 5. No one on staff knows much about action research, although you do. How would you go about establishing an action research team and project?

• You've formed a decision-making curriculum committee who reports that they would like to purchase a specific book series for Grade 6. The committee members, having done their research, feel strongly about their decision. You've had previous experience with this book series while you were an assistant principal in another district. From your experience, you've noticed several severe limitations of the series. What would you do?

• You've formed a leadership committee that has, in the past, functioned quite well. After the most recent faculty elections, two new members join the committee. You notice, and hear from others, that arguments are now common in most meetings. What would you do or suggest?

• You're a newly assigned principal to a high school that never experiences teacher leadership, to any significant degree, nor shared decision making. You want to establish a collaborative school environment. What would be your two-year plan to achieve your goal?

• You've successfully implemented shared decision making involving instructional and curricular matters. The leadership team informs you that they now would like decision-making power over personnel matters as well. How would you react?

Reproducible #8. Assessing Your Role in Teamwork

SA = Strongly Agree ("For the most part, yes.")
A = Agree ("Yes, but . . .")
D = Disagree ("No, but . . .")
SD = Strongly Disagree ("For the most part, no.")

SA	A	D	SD	1. I am willing to listen to and learn from others.
SA	A	D	SD	2. I am willing to alter my views after deliberating with others, if their views are more convincing.
SA	A	D	SD	3. I am willing to let go of a firmly held belief in order to reach consensus with others.
SA	A	D	SD	4. Although I am ultimately responsible for what happens in my school, I believe that responsibility is a shared goal of the entire team.
SA	A	D	SD	5. I intentionally serve as a collaborative leader.
SA	A	D	SD	6. If every other member of the team votes for "X" but I really believe in "Y," I would still go along with the team if I could not convince them otherwise.
SA	A	D	SD	7. I am not willing to relinquish my authority for the good of a team concept.
SA	A	D	SD	8. Team members should like one another.
SA	A	D	SD	9. Everyone on a team should participate.
SA	A	D	SD	10. My role on the team is to ensure that conflict is minimized.
SA	A	D	SD	11. Establishing clear goals and roles for each member is imperative.
SA	A	D	SD	12. Team-building activities should be used to establish good working relationships among team members.
SA	A	D	SD	13. Consensus is a much better way of reaching a conclusion than voting.
SA	A	D	SD	14. A team member should always remain on a team even when personal conflicts reach crisis proportions.
SA	A	D	SD	15. Collaboration is among the most important things I do as principal.

Analyze your responses:

The following "answers" are suggestive, because no survey can accurately assess your commitment to collaboration. However, these responses can serve as a basis of comparison and as a means of reflection by yourself or with a colleague.

An affirmative response to the following items is clearly necessary if collaboration is going to work in your school: 1 through 7, 11 through 13, and 15.

Reproducible #9. Assessing Your Role in Action Research

This questionnaire is a bit different from the others in this volume and series in that it assesses your knowledge of action research very specifically or technically. You can, of course, support action research initiatives, as principal, without having specialized expertise in the area, but having some basic knowledge and experience in actually conducting it is more likely to strengthen your commitment. Please complete this questionnaire as a means of self-reflection or analysis in order to assess the extent to which you are knowledgeable of the action research process. Note that the questionnaire stresses knowledge that is not matched to the content of this book; it's just meant to prompt you to think about what you know or may not know about research specifics. You know, though, that it is really only "doing" action research a bit that will assist you to gain greater familiarity and knowledge. Please note that the questions posed do not cover all areas of action research. The intent is to conduct some rudimentary assessment. Refer to any good text on educational or action research for details (see Resource E in this book). Please also note that your responses are private. Your honest responses to the following items will best serve as reflective tools to assist you in becoming an even better collaborative leader.

1. Which of the following is an example of empirical research?
   a. A study of the impact of a literature-based reading series on the attitudes of fifth graders toward reading
   b. A review of the literature on cooperative learning
   c. A historical overview of homeschooling
   d. All of these are examples of empirical research

2. Which is an example of an ethnographic study?
   a. Images of principals in the media
   b. Relationship between math and science scores among 11th graders
   c. A day in the life of a local school superintendent
   d. Programmed textbook instruction versus computer-assisted instruction

3. Mr. Solomon is a principal in an elementary school. Mr. Jones, a sixth-grade teacher, complains that one student, Billy, is disruptive and recalcitrant. Mr. Solomon tells the teacher to record Billy's behavior in anecdotal form for two weeks before scheduling a conference with the guidance counselor. During the first week, Mr. Jones discovers that Billy acts out 26 times. During the second week, he acts out 22 times. During the third week, Mr. Jones meets with the guidance counselor to work out Billy's problems. The counselor sets up a special reward system for Billy. During the fourth week, Billy acts out 18 times. During the fifth week, the disturbances decrease to only five times. Mr. Jones and the counselor conclude that the technique used with Billy is successful. What research design was employed?
   a. Pre-test–post-test control group design
   b. Control group–only design
   c. Interrupted time series design
   d. Single measurement design
   e. Nonequivalent control group design

4. Mrs. James teaches computers at P.S. 999 in New York. She has a new programmed instruction textbook that she wishes to use with her classes. She decides to test the effectiveness of the new textbook. She chooses two classes that rank similarly in ability on a pretest in computer literacy. She gives her programmed text to group A, but with group B she continues her normal instruction. At the end of the semester, she gives a test on computer knowledge and discovers that the class using the new text outperformed the other group (group B). She concludes that the new text should be incorporated in all the classes. What research design did Mrs. James use?
   a. Nonequivalent design
   b. Interrupted time series design

c. Pre-test–post-test design
d. Pre-test–post-test control group design
e. Control group–only design

5. You take 50 fourth-grade students and assign 25 randomly to one class and 25 randomly to the other class. Both groups are measured beforehand. Two different treatments are presented, then a follow-up measurement is given. Which type of design is this?
a. Pre-test–post-test control group design
b. Pre-test–post-test only design
c. One-shot case study
d. Nonequivalent control group design
e. One-group pre-test–post-test design

6. A quasi-experimental design involving one group that is repeatedly pretested, exposed to an experimental treatment, and repeatedly post-tested is known as a
a. Pre-test–post-test design
b. Post-test–only design
c. Time-series design
d. Revolving series design
e. None of these

7. Classify the following study:
Research hypothesis: Achievement in Spanish is affected by class size.
Procedure: At the beginning of the school year, the students in Highpoint High School are randomly assigned to one of two types of Spanish classes: a class with 20 or fewer students or a class of 40 or more. The two groups are compared at the end of the year on Spanish achievement.
a. Historical
b. Descriptive
c. Correlational
d. Experimental

8. Janice Barnett, Supervisor of Curriculum, wanted to evaluate a new reading series that her district was considering. She decided to study fifth graders in a particular school. She selected one class of fifth-grade students who were introduced to the new reading series. Another comparable fifth-grade class would use the "old" reading series. At the end of the year, Ms. Barnett tested all students in reading comprehension. What type of study is this?
a. Pre-test–post-test control group
b. Nonequivalent
c. Case study
d. Historical

9. To determine if a particular textbook is appropriate for a fifth-grade class, your analysis would entail which type of research?
a. Content analysis
b. Ethnography
c. Case study
d. Naturalism
e. Simulation

10. The major purpose of using an interview protocol is to:
a. Offer respondents a way to participate in the interview without having the interviewer present
b. Increase the chances that the respondent will respond honestly
c. Be able to conduct the interview in case the interviewer is not present
d. Provide the interviewer with a set of guidelines for conducting the interview

11. You are a principal in an intermediate school with a population of 750 students. As indicated by recent districtwide tests, student reading achievement has increased. You are interested in discovering how well the students in your school perform in reading compared to students in other schools throughout the country. Which of the following instruments of measurement would you use?
    a. A classroom achievement test
    b. Observation
    c. Examination of school records
    d. A questionnaire
    e. A standardized test

12. When a group of subjects sense that they are part of an experiment and react in a special way it is known as the
    a. John Henry effect
    b. Norton's Law
    c. Halo effect
    d. Hawthorne effect
    e. Pearson r

13. This is an ethical principle related to conducting research that ensures that participants in research are informed accurately about the general topic under investigation as well as any unusual procedures that may be used in the study.
    a. Accurate disclosure
    b. Fair-mindedness
    c. Ethics
    d. Beneficence

14. This occurs when subjects in the control group know they are, in a sense, competing with some other group (experimental) and, consequently, expend extra effort to perform better than the experimental group.
    a. Hawthorne effect
    b. John Henry effect
    c. Western Electric effect
    d. John James effect
    e. All of the above

15. Participant observation is frequently used in conducting
    a. Correlational research
    b. Ex post facto research
    c. Ethnographic research
    d. Quasi-experimental research

16. A research hypothesis should be stated in the form of a
    a. Value judgment
    b. Hypothetical construct
    c. Research question
    d. Predictive statement

17. The degree to which a test consistently measures whatever it measures is
    a. Reliability
    b. Validity
    c. Coefficient
    d. Statistical analysis
    e. None of these

18. Which of the following is the best example of an "unobtrusive instrument"?
    a. Supervisor walks into class for an on-the-spot observation
    b. Supervisor peeks into window of classroom without letting the teacher see him or her

c. Supervisor determines staff morale by examining the quantity and pattern of staff attendance

d. Interviewing teachers

e. Anonymous questionnaire

19. Internal validity is to accuracy of results as external validity is to
    a. Threats to validity
    b. Causality realities
    c. Triangulation
    d. Generalizability

20. What should be your first reaction when you hear a radio commentator report that a recently published article indicates that a particular drug may reduce the risks for cancer?
    a. Disbelieve the study
    b. Accept it as accurate
    c. Assume that it's a PR push by a pharmaceutical company
    d. Consider study limitations

21. Action research differs most from typical professional practice in its
    a. Concern for fostering students' learning
    b. Concern for discovering generalizable knowledge
    c. Promotion of practitioners' professional development
    d. Systematic collection of data as a guide to improving practice

22. List five benefits of conducting action research.

23. List the four basic steps of conducting action research.

24. List the three forms of action research.

25. List some practical guidelines or advice you would give others for conducting action research.

Reproducible #10. Assessing Your Role in Shared Decision Making

SA = Strongly Agree ("For the most part, yes.")
A   = Agree ("Yes, but . . .")
D   = Disagree ("No, but . . .")
SD = Strongly Disagree ("For the most part, no.")

SA   A   D   SD   1. I am in favor of building a school culture and environment that is conducive to teacher leadership, including both formal structures and informal behaviors.

SA   A   D   SD   2. I am willing to relinquish authority, trust teachers, empower teachers, include others, protect teacher leaders from their colleagues, share responsibility for failure, and give credit for success.

SA   A   D   SD   3. I believe that the role of the principal should be redefined from instructional leader to developer of a community of leaders.

SA   A   D   SD   4. I intend to create opportunities for teachers to lead; build professional learning communities; provide quality, results-driven professional development; and celebrate innovation and teacher expertise.

SA   A   D   SD   5. I will provide a school environment in which teachers engage in reflective practice and can implement ideas that grow from reflection.

SA   A   D   SD   6. I will pay attention to the change process and to human relationships, listen well, communicate respect, perpetuate ongoing dialogue about teaching and learning, and encourage teachers to act on shared visions.

SA   A   D   SD   7. I will empower teachers as leaders.

SA   A   D   SD   8. I am truly interested in bringing others into decision-making processes.

SA   A   D   SD   9. I fully understand the purpose for collaborating.

SA   A   D   SD   10. I will establish a conducive, nonthreatening environment in which to conduct decision-making deliberations.

SA   A   D   SD   11. I will open lines of communication to all those interested in partaking in decision making.

SA   A   D   SD   12. I am ready, willing, and able to introduce, when needed, conflict-resolution strategies.

SA   A   D   SD   13. I will be highly visible, cordial, and knowledgeable in regard to shared decision making.

SA   A   D   SD   14. I intend to establish the necessary time and space structures that are so necessary for collaboration to take place.

SA   A   D   SD   15. I remain committed to shared decision making as a way to support collaboration in my school.

Part VI

Book Six:
What Every Principal Should Know About Operational Leadership

Overview of Operational Leadership: Discover Best Practices for Implementing Efficient School Management

Although principals may understandably devote a great deal of attention to supporting the cultural and instructional needs of their schools, the core administrative challenge remains: managing the school's personnel, facilities, and financial resources. As the sixth volume of the seven-part series, *What Every Principal Should Know About Operational Leadership* provides an essential tool for new and veteran principals who want to run their school sites more efficiently and intentionally every day of the school year. Filled with best practice examples, resources, and implementation ideas, this guide also includes the following features:

- Insightful questionnaire and response analysis (TAKE THE SURVEY NOW on pages xiii–xv.)
- Case study with reflective questions (READ THE CASE STUDY NOW and answer the reflective questions on pages 12–15.)
- "What You Should Know About" sections framing each chapter
- Self-assessment for determining effectiveness of operational leaders

Best Practices in Getting Organized

Overview

This chapter covers three important areas for getting organized. A principal may possess enormous knowledge and instructional skills. But without developing organizational skills their effectiveness will be jeopardized. How do principals balance the myriad amount of work necessary to accomplish their objectives? What skills are necessary? Effective principals as operational leaders should know something about each of these areas that have an impact on their success:

- **Eight Organizational Tips**—We discuss Simon and Newman's (2004) suggestions to enhance organizational skills.
- **Preparing the Schedule**—We review some suggestions for learning how to schedule.
- **Managing Time**—This section provides specific suggestions from several authorities on getting the most out of time.

Discussion Questions

1. How do you find the time to do all that must be done in such a chaotic environment?

2. What criteria do you use to prioritize tasks?

3. How would you rate your organizational skills?

4. How would others assess your organizational skills?

5. Have you done anything to help yourself in this area? Explain.

6. What organizational tips would you offer a new principal? (See Subsection 1 in the chapter.)

7. Who taught you to do scheduling?

8. What techniques or strategies work for you in scheduling events and programs? (See Subsection 2 in the chapter.)

9. What concrete suggestions could you offer to manage time most efficiently and effectively? (See Subsection 3 in the chapter.)

Engagement Activity

Time: 20 minutes

Materials: *What Every Principal Should Know About Operational Leadership* by Jeffrey Glanz

Utilizing the scenario presented on pages 16–17 about Ms. Rodriguez's hectic schedule, lead the group in a discussion of how hectic life is as a principal. Using the whip-around technique, have each participant share his or her hectic schedule, challenges, and personal strategies for "getting the job done."

As a follow-up activity, reproduce each of the quotations in the chapter and have participants share what each quote means to them.

Best Practices in Managing Facilities

Overview

One of the most thankless jobs in a school is managing facilities. Time consuming, even annoying, taking care that all facilities are operational is an important responsibility of a principal. Principals may oversee a team of custodians or others, but ultimately it is the principal who is responsible for a smoothly running organization. This chapter covers four major ideas that all principals should take into consideration:

> - **Coordinating Safety and Security**—Marzano's (2003) five action steps for an orderly school environment are discussed, as are other primary aspects of safety and security.
> - **Overseeing the Cafeteria**—This section provides an outline of ideas related to the many aspects of cafeteria management.
> - **Working With the Custodian**—We discuss selected suggestions for working well with the custodian.
> - **Conducting a Facilities Evaluation**—This section provides a checklist to consider when conducting such an evaluation.

Discussion Questions

1. What training did you receive in terms of facilities management in graduate school?

2. How do you ensure a safe and secure school facility?

3. How much time does it take to address facilities management?

4. Who's in charge of ordering supplies and how do you ensure that the correct supplies are ordered, catalogued, and kept safely in the school (to avoid theft, etc.)?

5. Describe your custodial staff. How do they support your work in this area? What problems have you encountered with the custodian, if any? Explain.

6. What suggestions would you make for coordinating safety and security in your school? (See Subsection 1 in the chapter.)

7. How do you run the cafeteria? Describe in detail. (See Subsection 2 in the chapter.)

8. What suggestions would you make to a new principal for working well with the custodian? (See Subsection 3 in the chapter.)

9. What process have you established for evaluating school facilities? (See Subsection 4 in the chapter.)

Engagement Activity

Time: 30 minutes

Materials: *What Every Principal Should Know About Operational Leadership* by Jeffrey Glanz

Conduct a whole group discussion of "custodian" stories.

As a follow-up activity, use DeRoche's (1987) principles on pages 33–37 to lead a discussion of specific facilities management issues.

Best Practice in School Finance and Handling the Budget

Overview

Many principals around the country are responsible for managing all aspects of the school budget and all school finance issues. In New York City for instance, principals are given complete authority over budget and finance and are then held responsible for expenditure choices made. Although fairly rigid procedures are in place for these expenditures, principals, not central office or regional officials, are in charge. This chapter addresses, in brief, important fiscal matters.

Discussion Questions

1. Where did you learn about budgetary matters?

2. Assess your knowledge of budget and finance. What knowledge do you lack?

3. What budgetary clarification systems are in place in your district?

4. To whom, if anybody, do you delegate fiscal matters?

5. How do you make budgetary decisions when various factions in the school require additional revenues?

Engagement Activity

Time: 30 minutes

Materials: chart paper, markers, masking tape, *What Every Principal Should Know About Operational Leadership* by Jeffrey Glanz

Refer to the "What You Should Know About School Finance and Handling the Budget" section on pages 58–61. Review the PPBS five-step process on page 58 with the group and lead the group in a discussion regarding the many budgetary and financial bullets on pages 58 and 59.

As a follow-up activity, conduct a role-playing session between a central office finance officer and a school building principal. The central office official states that monies have been misspent. What arguments and pieces of evidence can a principal bring to back her or his case?

Best Practices in Human Resources Management

Overview

Human resources management, or working with people, is a huge part of a principal's work. Working with and managing people is critical to a principal's success. Principals who see themselves as managers of operations and deal exclusively with administrative aspects of the job will ultimately fail. A principal needs to be a people person. A principal must possess key human relations skills. Under the rubric of human resources, a host of other responsibilities are also necessary. This chapter covers seven major aspects of human resources management:

- **Recruiting, Inducting, and Retaining Good Teachers**—Learn from Alicia Kaelber and her commitment to best practices in teaching.
- **Evaluating Personnel and Programs**—Learn how Donald Toscano goes about evaluating personnel and programs in his building.

- **Working With the Union**—Learn Dominec Reno's suggestions for working with the union.
- **Dealing With Conflict**—Learn how Nazim Selovic deals with conflict.
- **Working With Your Assistant Principal**—Learn how Ronald Davis works with his three APs.
- **Attending to Legal Mandates**—Learn about the suggestions offered to Fernando Montalvo by his mentor.
- **Promoting In-Classroom and Schoolwide Positive Student Behavior**—Learn Teresa Radzik's advice for supporting appropriate student behavior schoolwide.

Discussion Questions

1. Do you like to interact with people or do you prefer to be alone reading a good book? Explain.

2. What does human resources management mean to you?

3. In your opinion, which is most important, the needs of the individual teacher or the requirements of the organization? Explain.

4. What does Abraham Maslow's needs hierarchy have to do with human resources management? (See pages 64–65.)

5. What strategies have you seen employed to recruit new teachers? (See Subsection 1 of the chapter.)

6. What strategies have you seen employed to induct teachers? (See Subsection 1.)

7. What strategies have you seen employed to retain teachers? (See Subsection 1.)

8. What does human resources management have to do with program evaluation? (See Subsection 2.)

9. How might you conduct a program evaluation? (See Subsection 2.)

10. Why is establishing good rapport with union officials so critical to your success as principal? (See Subsection 3.)

11. Can you suggest three ways of working well with union officials? (See Subsection 3.)

12. How do you personally deal with conflict among personnel? (See Subsection 4.)

13. What strategies would you employ to resolve personnel conflicts? Be specific. (See Subsection 4.)

14. What duties do you assign to your assistant principal? (See Subsection 5.)

15. Are you aware of legal issues that impact your work? Explain. (See Subsection 6.)

16. Have you established a schoolwide approach or system for managing discipline in your school? Explain. (See Subsection 7.)

Engagement Activity

Time: 40 minutes

Materials: chart paper, markers, masking tape, *What Every Principal Should Know About Operational Leadership* by Jeffrey Glanz

Refer to the "What You Should Know About Human Resources Management" section on pages 66–90. Ask participants to skim through pages 67–90 to select one subsection. Once they have selected preferred sections, divide them into like groups. Have group members assign a facilitator and recorder. The facilitator leads group members in an open discussion about the value of the suggestions offered in the section while they provide examples from their experience to indicate what has worked particularly well and what has not. A recorder will write down on chart paper all strategies generated by the group that have been successful. After 20 minutes of group work, reconvene and have each group report out.

As a follow-up activity, conduct a role-playing session for each scenario (solicit volunteers to play roles):

- Mentoring a first-year teacher who is intelligent and enthusiastic but who is having difficulty with classroom management
- Meeting with a union official over a grievance
- Resolving a dispute between two office secretaries
- Informing your AP that you expect her support at least in public and that you didn't appreciate her critical remarks made in front of the P.T.A.
- Receiving a call from an attorney saying that a parent is suing you personally for not removing her child from a class in which he was badly beat up
- Confronting fifth-grade teachers who do not want to comply with what they perceive as a schoolwide disciplinary policy that "favors students"

As a follow-up activity, have the group brainstorm strategies, techniques, and ideas for supporting teachers in your school building.

Best Practices in Communicating Effectively

Overview

This chapter reviews some strategies and techniques for improving listening and communication skills. The chapter also includes other suggestions for enhancing good communication verbally, in written fashion, and in social interactions. The important point here is that operational leadership is much more than organizing school files, setting up multicultural fairs, writing budget plans, and reading standard operations manuals. Operational leadership implies real action. Action inevitably occurs in close work with people. Communication is a principal's most valuable resource. Effective principals as operational leaders should know something about each of these areas:

- **Develop Listening Skills**—Practice an exercise to improve listening skills.
- **Communication Techniques**—Practice an exercise to enhance communication.
- **Avoid Barriers to Communication**—Learn to identify and avoid barriers to communication.
- **Use Assertion Messages**—Learn to use Bolton's (1986) assertion messages.
- **Keil's Six Essential Questions for Communicating for Results**—This section provides practical suggestions for principals drawn from the work of Keil (2005).

- **Simon and Newman's (2004) Five Suggestions for Enhancing Communication**—This section provides more commonsense suggestions for principals from Simon and Newman.
- **Use E-mail**—Here are some simple suggestions for using and not using e-mail.
- **Run Effective Meetings**—Learn these simple guidelines for a common way to communicate during a meeting.

Discussion Questions

1. What strategies do you use to enhance communication among staff?

2. Are you a good listener? What evidence can you bring to support your assertion?

3. What is the single most important strategy you would share with a first-year principal for developing listening skills?

4. Which of Keil's essential questions for communication makes the most sense to you? (See Subsection 5.)

5. Which of Simon and Newman's suggestions for enhancing communication makes the most sense to you? (See Subsection 6.)

6. Do you overuse e-mail as a means of communicating with staff? Explain. (See Subsection 7.)

7. What are a few suggestions you would offer a new principal for running meetings? (See Subsection 8.)

Engagement Activity

Time: 40 minutes

Materials: *What Every Principal Should Know About Operational Leadership* by Jeffrey Glanz

Refer to the "What You Should Know About Communicating Effectively" section on pages 94–102. Divide the group into triads with one person serving as observer and feedback monitor. The other two role-play principal and teacher. The principal is supervising this teacher with five years' experience in the classroom. Take notice of listening skills used and communication techniques used (verbal and non-verbal). Did the principal display any of the barriers to communication? Describe the use of assertion messages.

As a follow-up activity, have participants brainstorm verbal and non-verbal messages that miscommunicate.

Best Practices in Personal Management

Overview

This chapter covers two basic yet important matters related to personal management. The fundamental premise of this chapter is that a principal cannot serve effectively to help others without developing personal mastery. Effective principals as operational leaders should know something about:

> • **Dealing With Stress**—Suggestions for handling stress are discussed.
> • **Striving for Personal Renewal**—A variety of suggestions for addressing personal renewal are offered.

Discussion Questions

1. What stresses you most about your position?

2. How do you deal with stress?

3. What advice might you offer a colleague for dealing with the pressures and challenges of the principalship?

4. React to the four suggestions offered on pages 114–121 for dealing with stress. Which makes the most sense to you?

5. How do you renew yourself? Is it effective? How do you know?

6. What resources might you need to help you?

Engagement Activity

Time: 20 minutes

Materials: Any relaxation script
As a follow-up activity, facilitate a discussion about personal renewal strategies.

Culminating Activity

Time: 60–90 minutes

Materials: This culminating activity utilizes Resources A and B in *What Every Principal Should Know About Operational Leadership* by Jeffrey Glanz.

Divide the participants into two groups. One group will work on Resource A and the other group will work on Resource B. Make sure to provide copies of each Resource to each group (only one for each group, not one copy for each member because the group participation of all members will be enhanced by giving only one copy for the group). Allow groups to assign responsibilities to members:

Recorder—person responsible for recording info for group

Monitor—ensures that each group member participates (e.g., in the case of a silent member, the monitor might ask, "Steve, what do you think?" or "Do we all agree on the solution?")

Captain—ensures group stays on task to complete assigned task

Reporter—reports out to large group at end of session (may be one or two individuals)

What other roles/responsibilities can you encourage?

Resource A

Select as many in-basket simulations as time permits and brainstorm three specific strategies for coping/dealing with each scenario. Ensure all group members agree on each strategy (prioritize them here as relevant). During the report out phase, rather than just reading the scenario and reporting strategies, the group should first encourage audience reaction and participation and then share group strategies.

Resource B

Members administer the survey to the entire group. In other words, all session participants take the survey anonymously. Group members then tabulate results for later presentation and discussion. Afterwards, Resource B group members offer their personal insights to questionnaire items. For instance, someone might share that she doesn't really feel comfortable giving workshops to teachers in a particular area. Discussion should occur within a collegial, non-threatening, and supportive environment that encourages alternate ways of seeing things and offers positive, constructive suggestions. During the reporting out session, group members should plan, in advance, key questions to provoke audience participation.

Operational Leadership Reproducibles

Reproducible #1. Questionnaire

Directions: Using the following Likert scale, circle the answer that best represents your on-the-spot belief about each statement.

SA = Strongly Agree ("For the most part, yes.")
A = Agree ("Yes, but . . .")
D = Disagree ("No, but . . .")
SD = Strongly Disagree ("For the most part, no.")

SA   A   D   SD   1. Leading and managing are essential requirements for the principalship, but they address very different purposes.

SA   A   D   SD   2. I feel uncomfortable with theories involving administration, because they are often disconnected from practice.

SA   A   D   SD   3. Leadership is essentially a higher calling than management.

SA   A   D   SD   4. Principals should attend to both the operational and educational aspects of the job with equal vigor and attention.

SA   A   D   SD   5. Research indicates that principals, especially new ones, retain their jobs because of their managerial role but would rather delegate management functions to others so that they could devote more time to instructional leadership.

6. Examine the list of duties below that reflect some of the topics discussed in this book. First, rank them in terms of what you think you and your assistant principal(s) (APs) *actually* do in schools (i.e., award a #1 to the duty you think you or they do most frequently, #2 for the next most frequent duty, etc.). Second, rank them according to what is, in your view, their degree of importance (i.e., give a #1 to the duty principals and APs *should* be engaged in, a #2 to the next important duty, etc. Of course, your rankings may differ for APs). Compare your responses to the discussion in the answer section.

Student discipline

Lunch duty

School scheduling (coverages*)

Ordering textbooks

Parental conferences

Assemblies

Administrative duties

Articulation**

Evaluation of teachers

Student attendance

Emergency arrangements

Instructional media services

Counseling pupils

School clubs and the like

Assisting P.T.A.

Formulating goals

Staff development (inservice)

Faculty meetings

Teacher training

Instructional leadership

Public relations

Curriculum development

Innovations and research

School budgeting

Teacher selection

* The term *coverages* refers to scheduling substitute teachers to cover for absent regular classroom teachers.

** *Articulation* refers to the administrative and logistical duties required to prepare for graduation (e.g., preparing and sending cumulative record cards for graduating fifth graders to the middle school).

Before we analyze your responses, consider the importance of operational leadership. Running a school takes much effort, determination, and skill. As an operational leader you:

- Organize all school activities
- Establish widely known and accepted procedures for conducting business
- Coordinate programs and training activities
- Evaluate programs and personnel
- Prepare and oversee school and program schedules
- Manage physical plant and facilities
- Work closely with custodial, cafeteria, and office staff
- Prepare financial reports
- Assume responsibility for fiscal and budgetary integrity
- Recruit teachers
- Monitor teacher induction and mentoring
- Communicate

As you consider these responsibilities and many related others, share your thoughts about the questions in the questionnaire with a colleague.

Reproducible #2. Quotations

Examine these quotations about operational leadership. What do they mean to you?

"The choice is not whether a principal is leader or manager but whether the two emphases are in balance and, indeed, whether they complement each other."

—Thomas J. Sergiovanni

"Measures must focus attention on elements of systems that people believe can make a difference in the results toward which the system is managed."

—Phillip C. Schlechty

"Educational administrators are frequently expected to take on the roles of educational superperson, technical manager, and democratic leader."

—Cherry A. McGee Banks

"Leaders are people who do the right thing; managers are people who do things right."

—Warren Bennis

"Management is problem-oriented. Leadership is opportunity-oriented. Management works the system. Leadership works on the system."

—Stephen Covey

"Management is about human beings. Its task is to make people capable of joint performance, to make their strengths effective and their weaknesses irrelevant."

—Peter Drucker

"The principal is ultimately responsible for almost everything that happens in school and out."

—Roland S. Barth

"Leadership literature frequently gives the impression that managerial functions or responsibilities are less important than the leadership functions or responsibilities. Principals usually want to be instructional leaders. However, management and leadership responsibilities go hand in hand."

—Harvey B. Alvy and Pam Robbins

"The role of the principal as manager is key in the daily organizing, functioning, and execution of numerous processes and tasks that permit a school to accomplish its goals as a learning community."

—Marsha Speck

"School leaders must first of all be skillful managers. . . . Whatever else a district may want from its leaders, managerial skill is essential; without it, no school leader will last long."

—Stuart C. Smith and Philip K. Piele

"The overlap between leadership and management is centered on how they both involve influencing a group of individuals in goal attainment."

—Peter G. Northouse

"Success is good management in action."

—William E. Holler

"Principals must continue to upgrade their effective management practices that keep students safe and public policies and funds appropriately addressed, even as they commit their primary energies to the issues of teaching and learning."

—William A. Owings and Leslie S. Kaplan

"With the additional stress of federal and state mandates, we need every effective tool we can find to help our school principals and classroom teachers meet the new challenges of the 21st century."

—Jim R. Watson

"Organizational life need not be an endless series of meetings run by Robert's Rules of Order. There can and should be excitement and energy there."

—Susan R. Komives, Nance Lucas, and Timothy R. McMahon

"Viewing schools as relationships linked together as circuits is useful in understanding the interconnectedness of human social organizations and how information flows through them."

—Randall B. Lindsey, Laraine M. Roberts, and Franklin CampbellJones

"'A manager is responsible for consistency of purpose and continuity to the organization. The manager is solely responsible to see that there is a future for the workers.' [It is our responsibility as a society to manage our schools so that almost all students get a high-quality education]."

—William Glasser, quoting W. Edwards Deming

"Every great manager I've ever interviewed has it. No matter what the situation, their first response is always to think about the individual concerned and how things can be arranged to help that individual experience success."

—Marcus Buckingham

"When we discuss the operations of the school, we mean the daily activities necessary to keep the school operating smoothly and efficiently."

—Elaine L. Wilmore

"Because organizations are complex, surprising, deceptive, and ambiguous, they are formidably difficult to understand and manage."

—Lee G. Bolman and Terrence E. Deal

"Organize the work, establish procedures, and identify a clear focus for the work so that you can achieve your goals."

—Barbara L. Brick and Marilyn L. Grady

"Doing a good job in leadership without ruining yourself in the process may be difficult if you are too much of a perfectionist or too much of a procrastinator."

—Donald Schumacher

"The principal has a key role in the planning and operation of the school facility."

—Thelbert L. Drake and William H. Roe

"From the earliest research to the present day, the principal's establishment and maintenance of a safe, orderly school environment has been identified as the most fundamental element of effectiveness."

—Kathleen Cotton

"Handling the business affairs of a school well provides a credibility to internal and external publics so that other less visible or measurable results can be achieved."

—Thelbert L. Drake and William H. Roe

"To manage the organizational and operational facets of the school effectively, it is essential to have appropriate resources."

—Elaine L. Wilmore

"Principals have to learn how to maintain records required by federal, state, and local laws including (but not limited to) finances, the instructional program, health, fire, food service, crisis procedures, and attendance. . . . Principals need to understand state and district policies and must manage these policies, procedures, and regulations at the school level."

—Harvey B. Alvy and Pam Robbins

"If a learning community is to reach its goals and meet the needs of its students, the budget development process and final budget must reflect its priorities for the school."

—Marsha Speck

"A budget is an estimate, an educated guess, about revenue (income streams) and expenditures (disbursements of cash resources). That's all it is."

—John A. Black and Fenwick W. English

"School administrators are expected to know the law. The courts will not accept ignorance of the law as a defense."

—Dennis R. Dunklee and Robert J. Shoop

"Human resource theorists argue that the central task of managers is to build organizations and management systems that produce harmony between the needs of the individual and the needs of the organization."

—Lee G. Bolman and Terrence E. Deal

"Success typically requires a comprehensive strategy undergirded by a long-term human resource management philosophy."

—Lee G. Bolman and Terrence E. Deal

"Traditional bureaucratic approaches to organization and the newer approaches that emphasize the human dimensions of organization exist side by side and often compete for the attention and loyalty of educational administrators."

—Robert G. Owens

"Organizations need leaders who send clear, coherent, consistent, and appropriate messages."

—Joyce Kaser, Susan Mundry, Katherine E. Stiles, and Susan Loucks-Horsley

"True communication occurs when the listener hears what the sender intends."

—Rodney J. LaBrecque

"When people engage in effective communication with one another, they authentically share information and construct meaning together."
—Randall B. Lindsey, Laraine M. Roberts, and Franklin CampbellJones

"The principalship is a 'people' profession, and no degree of expertise in instructional, curricular, budgetary, or time management skills is going to make principals successful if they lack the ability to communicate honestly with students, faculty, classified staff, parents, and the broader community."
—Harvey B. Alvy and Pam Robbins

"All principals, regardless of experience, level of school, size of school, type of school district . . . have very important, difficult, and demanding jobs."
—John C. Daresh

"Principals must take care of themselves in order to care for others."
—Pam Robbins and Harvey B. Alvy

"Leaders know themselves; they know their strengths and nurture them."
—Warren Bennis

Reproducible #3. Forms of Leadership

Instructional

School-Community

Collaborative

Strategic

Ethical-Spiritual

Cultural

OPERATIONAL LEADERSHIP

THE FOUNDATION

Reproducible #4. Working With Your AP

Tips include:

- Realize that each AP has something unique to offer the school.
- Discover the talent of each AP.
- Capitalize on the unique talents of each AP.
- Assign APs a grade level or responsibilities that will challenge them but will also give them the opportunity to succeed.
- Meet with them collectively as part of your cabinet, but also afford time for each one to see or meet with you privately.
- Realize that they are your "assistants," and as such, they are there to carry out your policies and to take leadership responsibilities in the areas you delegate to them.
- Listen to them, and solicit their advice regularly.
- Don't show favoritism to one over the other.
- Don't talk about one to another, especially in a negative way.
- Protect and support your APs.
- Understand and accommodate your AP's leadership style.
- Remain assertive by asking them to assume leadership responsibilities in special areas.
- Assign each of them managerial duties to help alleviate your burdens, but don't give them work you would never do.
- Do not make any major decision without seeking the assistance or advice of your APs.
- Praise them in public, and chastise them if necessary in private, individually.
- Remain honest by openly sharing your views of instructional improvement with your APs.
- Remain honest by openly sharing your views of management with your APs.
- Never criticize or question the authority of your AP in public.
- Offer to assist your AP in instructional, curricular, and administrative matters.
- Understand your APs' strengths and limitations, and offer to assist where and when necessary.
- Remain steadfast in your beliefs and share them with your APs.
- Offer to cover a lunch duty or some other mundane administrative assignment from time to time.
- Let them represent you at various district forums, when appropriate.
- Offer concrete proposals to maximize their performance.
- Share teacher views with the APs.
- Seek, in private, a rationale for their decisions.
- Respectfully demand their allegiance and loyalty to you, because you are ultimately responsible to the parents and children you serve.
- Serve as a mentor for them.
- Encourage innovative thinking.
- Encourage the advancement of their careers.
- Always see them as partners, your assistants.

Reproducible #5. Suggestions for Balancing Management With Leadership

• Assess your ability to manage a school and your belief that leading your school is most imperative.

• Affirm that both leadership and management are essential and must be attended to daily in order to achieve success as a principal.

• Envision in both theory and practice that management and leadership are two sides of one coin and that you should therefore utilize your management skills to further leadership goals.

• Affirm the preceding vision by "supporting" leadership initiatives through "management efforts" that include money, personnel, time, and information (Matthews & Crow, 2003, pp. 177–180).
   a. "Money" (p. 177): Attend to budgetary issues to support reform initiatives such as instructional improvement projects.
   b. "Personnel" (p. 179): Providing for and organizing workshops or professional development programs for all school personnel is necessary to support cultural, instructional, and strategic leadership.
   c. "Time" (p. 180): Attend to time management through intelligent and considerate scheduling, whether it's planning to free teachers to attend workshops or to provide for common prep periods so that groups of teachers may form leadership committees.
   d. "Information" (p. 180): Whether it's collecting information via the Internet to support the new schoolwide Balanced Literacy program to teach reading to fourth graders or incorporating data-driven decision making to inform classroom practice, you need to manage information in an efficient and organized manner.

• Furthermore, affirm the combination of management and leadership by attending to "planning" initiatives (Matthews & Crow, 2003, p. 182). Managing a strategic planning initiative is a tedious, yet important, responsibility as principal. Good management skills are required for short- and long-range planning. (See Principal Leadership Series volume on strategic planning.)

• You can also affirm the combination of management and leadership by "taking action" (Matthews & Crow, 2003, p. 184). There's a cute riddle or story I once heard: Three frogs are sitting on a log. Two decided to jump off. So how many are left? Answer: Three, because deciding to do something and actually doing so are two different things. We can plan to carry out our initiatives, but eventually we must actually implement them. Only someone who is well organized, makes efficient use of time, schedules appropriately, handles budgetary issues, attends to human resource exigencies, and fosters good communication will be able to take appropriate actions to move the school forward.

• Finally, management and leadership come together when you evaluate and assess your efforts. Good management skills are necessary for data collection, analysis, and interpretation. Assessment results can then be used to improve instruction in classrooms and schoolwide.

Reproducible #6. Realities of Operational Leadership: In-Basket Simulations

During an interview, you are asked to respond to the following scenarios:

• You are the newly appointed principal of an intermediate school in which the former principal never considered management-related problems or issues. She either ignored them or delegated them to others without checking on them. You feel the school is consequently "falling apart" because of her lack of attention to managerial responsibilities. What are the first steps you would take?

• Your superintendent informs you that several parents have registered formal complaints that the physical plant of your school is deteriorating under your watch. Bathrooms, they complain, are rarely cleaned promptly, and lightbulbs are rarely replaced in dark corners of the building. How do you respond?

• You are the new principal of a fairly large school. You find yourself involved in day-to-day school management and operational issues, but you can't seem to find time for your true interest and love, instructional improvement. How do you balance the two responsibilities?

• The IEP team needs your assistance, because they say they are receiving resistance from several teachers for including students with disabilities in their classrooms. You are cognizant of your role as principal to identify and refer students who might have a disability. You also affirm your role in due process for them and take part on the IEP team. You also know you must serve as a facilitator to help teachers accept these children in their classes. How would you go about accomplishing this? Explain the management strategies you might employ.

• You want to establish Collaborative Team Teaching (CTT) classes, but your faculty is resisting the idea. How would you go about staffing the CTT program? Describe how you would go about recruiting and selecting new faculty for your school.

• A teacher complains that she is being sexually harassed by a new teacher, Mr. Smith. What do you do?

• Your school has instituted a new Balanced Literacy program and the Workshop Model of instruction for all grades. You must incorporate block scheduling to facilitate such instructional efforts. How might you go about doing so, given you have never block-scheduled before?

• Mr. Schulenberg, the music chair, informs you that he needs a few new musical instruments, because several instruments have recently been damaged because of poor storage procedures. Not included in the annual budget that he submitted to you, these musical instruments are necessary in order for Mr. Schulenberg to prepare for the forthcoming schoolwide Music Fair at the high school. How do you rearrange the budget to accommodate his request?

• You've been informed by the central office that your instructional budget will be cut in half for the next academic year. You know you have planned several instructional initiatives that require additional funding. What do you do?

• How do you use technology as a management tool?

• What are some ways you can raise money for your school?

• A reporter from Channel 7 calls you to ask if she can come to your school tomorrow to interview students on school and neighborhood violence. What do you say?

• The gifted program in your school has been in effect for five years without ever having gone through a thorough evaluation for effectiveness. What steps would you take to evaluate this program? Describe them in detail, providing specific examples.

• How would you discipline an employee who has repeatedly reported to work late for a given month (consider the fact that his explanations for his lateness are non-existent or unsubstantiated)?

• If Jerry is continually late to work, although he may have a viable excuse in that his mother, whom he cares for on daily basis, is quite ill, his absence nevertheless has consequences for an orderly administration of the school day. Practically, his class needs coverage. Legal mandates require that students be supervised by licensed personnel. An added complication is that his students are losing out on valuable instructional time by his repeated tardiness or absences. Here's a case in which the organization requires adherence to standard procedures of operation (i.e., attendance policy), yet there are individual constraints (Jerry's need to care for his mother). As principal, you have to make a decision or take a course of action to address this problem. How would you handle this situation?

• How would you begin a process of firing a tenured teacher who verbally abuses his students (consider that you have complaints from parents and students, but you have never seen him behave this way)?

• A rumor spreads in your school that you are resigning. What steps would you take to dispel such rumors?

• A middle school student demands to take his medicine even though no parental consent form is on file, and the parent is unavailable. What would you do?

• Your secretary informs you that she just received a phone call from an anonymous caller saying a bomb will go off in 30 minutes. What do you do?

• Parents and community members complain that your school has no access for people in wheelchairs. They demand that you take action. What would or could you do?

• You discover that some equipment received last month (two VCRs and three DVD players) is missing. What do you do?

• What would you do to encourage teachers to trust that you are there to "help" them and not merely to "evaluate" them?

• How would you forge a role for yourself as an instructional leader and not merely a manager, especially in a school in which the former principal did not focus on instruction?

• How would you maximize all internal and external resources to maximize student learning in your school?

• What procedures and guidelines would you establish with the police and fire departments?

• How will you ensure that the school physical plant, equipment, and support systems are operating safely, efficiently, and effectively?

• There's no homework policy in your school. What steps would you take to establish a policy?

• You are a newly appointed principal who has been notified by the superintendent that each school must establish its own art education program. The superintendent wants you to establish and evaluate the program's effectiveness and to provide a full implementation plan within three months. Describe the steps you would take to establish and evaluate the program. Be sure to include goals and objectives, staffing considerations, criteria for selection, curriculum issues that need to be addressed, materials and resources needed, and so forth. Be as specific as you can.

• A parent calls you and accuses Mr. Henderson of hitting her child. She demands that you immediately dismiss the teacher. She doesn't like your response and threatens to come up to school to shoot you. What do you do?

• During an outdoor lunch period, a boy sustains a deep cut on his leg and is bleeding profusely. You happen on the scene. Describe in step-by-step fashion what you would do from beginning to end.

- The number of accidents in the school yard at lunchtime has increased dramatically. Indicate two immediate steps you would take for dealing with accidents in the yard. State how each step would contribute to safety in the yard.

- You receive complaints from parents via the telephone and letters about the incidence of pediculosis (head lice), which appears to be spreading rapidly throughout the school. Some parents are very angry, because their children become affected again after their condition has been cleared up. State four recommendations for immediate action you would make concerning the problem of pediculosis.

- A food fight breaks out during an indoor lunch lineup. You shout over the loudspeaker to no avail. Three lunch aides have not shown up yet. You are alone in the room with nearly 200 children, and about 15 of them are now throwing food. What do you do?

- A teacher reports that her purse is missing. It is five minutes prior to dismissal. She tells you she intends to strip-search the students. Then she hangs up the phone.

- You catch a custodian drinking alcohol on duty in the basement. What do you do?

- Children are bored during indoor lunch lineups. What varied activities can you plan to keep their attention and minimize misbehavior?

- Two secretaries, Ms. Valasquez and Ms. Haley, are in constant conflict over their duties. Set forth and justify the steps you would take to resolve the situation.

- Teachers in your middle school have complained that the dean awards treats to students sent to his office for disciplinary action. They complain to you that such rewards reinforce student misbehavior. The teachers demand action. What would you do?

- As a middle school principal sitting in your office speaking to a parent, you receive a phone call from a lunchroom aide who informs you: "Please come to the cafeteria as fast as you can. All the students are shouting that the food is terrible, and some are throwing their food and trays on the floor. We can't control them." Describe your immediate and long-term actions.

- As a new principal, you find there is no Standard Procedures Manual in your school. No guidelines ever existed for handling most logistical and administrative matters. Describe the steps you'd take to write such a manual and what you would include in the manual.

- You receive this e-mail from a parent:

Dear Mr. X,
My son Douglas is in Ms. Treacher's class. Yesterday, two boys in his class, Sam F. and Richard F., asked him for five dollars on the way home from school. Douglas told them he didn't have any money. They said they would beat him up if he didn't bring them the money today. I am keeping Douglas home until I can be sure of his safety.
Yours truly, Mrs. Jackson.

Describe your actions in detail.

- You have been a successful principal for 10 years. The superintendent calls you one afternoon and asks if you would serve as a mentor for three new principals. These new principals have no idea how to balance their duties of management with other leadership areas. What suggestions could you offer to these new principals? Offer at least 10 suggestions.

- How do you find time to renew yourself?

Reproducible #7. Assessing Your Role in Operational Leadership

Use the following abbreviations, and jot your response in the margin.

SA = Strongly Agree ("For the most part, yes.")
A = Agree ("Yes, but . . .")
D = Disagree ("No, but . . .")
SD = Strongly Disagree ("For the most part, no.")

As principal, I should be able to deal effectively with both the operational and educational aspects of the job.
    I really think it's unfair and not even possible to undertake both functions with excellent results.

It is not asking too much of a principal to deal with both the operational and educational aspects of the job.
    It is asking too much of a principal to deal with both the operational and educational aspects of the job.

I am ready to delegate responsibility to others to help do my job.
    I feel I must do it myself, or else it won't get done.

I believe I should personally oversee all phases of operations in my school.
    I believe that routine administrative matters should be handled by others who report to the principal, and only special and exceptional matters should be referred to the principal.

I personally plan the school's master schedule.
    I delegate that responsibility to my AP.

I do not delegate most administrative or logistical matters to my assistant principal so I can devote most of my time to instructional matters; I handle both equally.
    I delegate most administrative or logistical matters to my assistant principal so I can devote most of my time to instructional matters.

I designate room assignments personally.
    I give my AP that responsibility.

I ensure that school policies and procedures are in sync with district directives.
    I rarely consider district mandates and policies because most often they are irrelevant.

I personally examine student test score data in each major academic area.
    I have no time to do so.

I personally examine student attendance and tardiness rates to establish patterns of behavior and to develop strategies for dealing with problems.
    I have no time to do so; I delegate that responsibility.

I consult my school board on relevant and important managerial matters.
    I rarely bother them with such mundane matters.

I conduct and oversee lunch duty.
    I do not conduct lunch duty. I supervise it. My AP is there all the time.

I personally write the school's annual report.
    I delegate that responsibility to an AP.

I alert the staff to districtwide programs and new initiatives.
    I have no time to do so.

I write thank-you notes to my staff for jobs well done.
    I do so only once a year.

I distribute surveys to parents, teachers, staff, and students to ascertain how well my school is managed.
    I have never done so.

I work closely with the head custodian to ensure that major work and improvements are concluded in a timely fashion.
    Because I have no knowledge of custodial matters, I let the custodian carry on independently, reporting to me occasionally.

I inspect the school building roof.
    I never have done so.

I conduct a security walk-through on a daily basis.
    Perhaps I do so monthly.

I coordinate all school events, during and after school, with the custodian.
    I rarely do so in reality; I have no time.

I check on the availability of instructional materials in supply closets.
    I have a secretary do that.

I order new textbooks for different grades.
    I let teachers or APs do that.

I collect and monitor teacher attendance, grade, and lesson plan books.
    I rarely do that anymore; who has the time?

If I don't manage my school well, I can't lead effectively.
    I can still be an effective leader even though I care little about managerial matters, because in the end, they really handle themselves.

I am an efficient and effective manager.
    I am neither a very efficient nor a very effective manager.

I meet all district deadlines for reports, projects, and so on.
    I am a procrastinator, and they know it.

I pride myself on my good organizational skills.
    I need help in this area.

I have good time management skills.
    Time flies by; I have little time to do all that needs to be done.

I deal with stress well, under most circumstances.
    I am stressed out most of the time, especially as the day wears on.

I personally evaluate every worker in my building.
    Who has the time to do that? I "hit" the main people.

I know how to relax.
    I relax on weekends.

I realize that every action I take is seen and is being studied by others.
    I am unaware or simply don't care what others think.

I take my responsibility to hire and fire seriously.
    I have no control over either.

I am the most important person in the school in terms of setting the tone for good pupil behavior.
    The teacher is more important than I am.

I am aware of state and federal statutes as they relate to various legal issues facing life in schools (e.g., student searches, sexual harassment, drug testing, school prayer).
    I am legally inept.

I maintain eye contact with the person to whom I am speaking.
    I can't stand people. I prefer to interact infrequently.

I am familiar with most aspects of school law.
    I am somewhat familiar with most aspects of school law.

I conduct fair evaluations of my teachers.
    I give everyone a satisfactory grade, because it's impossible to remove an incompetent tenured teacher.

I wouldn't mind if teachers evaluated my work as principal.
    They have no right to evaluate me; I'm the boss.

I am good at managing conflict among staff members.
    I let people work out their own issues.

I take my role as manager seriously.
    I prefer to focus exclusively on non-managerial duties.

Although I am a manager, I realize that role is insufficient. In order to be effective, I must lead effectively as well.
> Although I am a leader, I realize that role is insufficient. In order to be effective, I must manage effectively as well.

I personally oversee the program to induct and mentor new teachers.
> Who has the time? My APs assist.

I am the only true leader in the building.
> Everyone can lead in different ways.

I am responsible for all budgetary items in my school.
> I wish I had no responsibility for budget.

I should be held accountable for any serious budgetary errors.
> The superintendent or central office should be accountable; I'm too busy.

I develop and oversee the school's strategic financial plan.
> My AP does that.

I ensure that transportation procedures for students in my school are well established.
> My AP ensures that transportation procedures for students in my school are well established.

I am well organized.
> I am generally disorganized, but that is OK because I have an AP who is very well organized.

I keep an orderly office.
> My office is a mess, and I prefer it that way.

I am generally on top of things.
> I am generally lost when it comes to managerial matters.

I rely only on myself.
> I tend to rely on others, too.

It is indeed possible to be a great manager and a great leader.
> It's impossible, and anyone who tells you it is possible is lying.

You cannot serve as an effective leader without needing to attend to managerial matters.
> You can serve as an effective leader without needing to attend too much to managerial matters.

I am conversant with all standard operational procedures in my school building.
> I rarely, if ever, refer to that manual.

I would not hesitate to ask a colleague or my superintendent for advice regarding managing my school.
> To be honest, I would be embarrassed to do that.

I oversee fire drills in my school.
    My AP does that, too.

I keep an eye on the exterior of my school building to ensure there's no graffiti or physical damage present.
    I rarely do that, because that should be the custodian's job.

I monitor hallway and bulletin board displays.
    My AP does that; I have no time because I am usually spending time completing reports for the district office.

I am an effective communicator to all community constituents.
    I don't communicate well; I prefer to manage from my office.

I review supply inventories for my school.
    I never do; my secretary handles those matters.

I balance my professional and personal lives well.
    I am a workaholic, and I rarely get a chance to care for myself.

I am able to prioritize tasks well.
    I get overwhelmed easily, so I take one task on at a time.

I need no help managing my school.
    I can use a mentor.

I'm a very good manager, but a poor instructional leader.
    I am a good instructional leader, but quite a disorganized manager.

I work well in chaos.
    I just can't stand disruptions.

I use technology to help me organize managerial tasks in school.
    I shy away from technology.

I can use technology in all its facets.
    Aside from e-mail, I really don't feel comfortable with much technology.

People usually understand me.
    People seem to continually misinterpret my motives.

I rarely get angry.
    I get angry frequently.

I am a good listener.
    I am a poor listener.

I am laid-back and easygoing. Managing my school is relatively easy.
    I am nervous over most managerial functions and matters.

I delegate just enough.
   I delegate too much.

I label documents carefully before I put them away.
   I rarely file anything; my secretary does most of it.

I can locate my paperwork easily.
   Papers usually get lost.

I complete most projects in a timely manner.
   Time seems to fly, and I rarely complete my projects on time.

I am a self-starter.
   It's hard to motivate myself at times.

I have enough principal colleagues I can confide in.
   I am a loner and prefer it that way.

When an incident occurs, I usually put it in writing as a form of documentation for possible later use.
   I usually forget to document such matters.

I meticulously keep anecdotals.
   I rarely record information myself or keep anecdotals.

Evaluation is necessary to ensure accountability.
   I have little time, so I give everyone a satisfactory grade.

Evaluation and supervision accomplish the same goal.
   They are different functions.

I manage conflict well.
   I avoid conflict at all costs.

I am in touch with the local fire department on a regular basis.
   Who has the time? I think I contacted them once in two years.

I communicate with local politicians as necessary regarding issues affecting my school.
   Who has the time?

I oversee all fire drills and provide appropriate training to the entire staff.
   My AP does.

I review child abuse laws and regulations with my staff.
   I don't do so, because they all know about these regulations already.

I oversee all equipment inventory in my school.
   Who has the time? My AP handles this for me.

I take pride in my managerial duties as principal.
    I hate my managerial duties.

I don't let my managerial responsibilities detract from leadership imperatives.
    They often do, though.

I am able to handle both managing and leading my school with facility and ease.
    I can't seem to get a handle on both functions.

I oversee all major purchases in my school.
    My secretary does that for me; who has the time?

I carefully monitor all budgetary items on my own.
    I delegate budget to my secretary, and she notifies me if anything major is needed.

Although I delegate budget to my assistant, I oversee all expenditures and related budgetary items.
    I delegate it all to my AP.

Well-established procedures exist for supply and equipment requisitions.
    I rarely have the time to monitor supply and equipment requisitions.

I handle taking inventory myself.
    I delegate and oversee inventorying.

I consult my faculty and staff before I purchase major instructional or other items.
    I don't bother them with administrative tasks.

I have had my school checked for asbestos.
    Oops.

My planned budget reflects the priorities for the school.
    I put together my budget regardless of school priorities, because there are items that transcend our goals and objectives.

I never make plans unless I consider school budget and resource allocation.
    I rarely consider school budget and resource allocation when planning.

I am ready to reallocate current resources, if needed, to reach our strategic goals.
    Once the budget is set, I will not make any changes.

I provide for accountability of a budget tied to student outcomes.
    I rarely consider student outcomes when it comes to budgeting.

Whenever we make copies, use postage, or repair audiovisual aids, I keep budgetary constraints in mind.
    I never do so.

I try to follow these steps in the budget process: Review budget data and standard operational procedures; tie budget to student learning; create a draft budget; share draft budget, collect feedback, and prepare final draft; implement budget; receive feedback on budget.
    I rarely do so.

I have a plan for inspecting the school plant and all facilities.
    I have too much to do to inspect facilities. I have the custodian do so, and then I consult with him or her as needed.

I regularly evaluate maintenance of my building.
    I have no time to manage maintenance of my building, because I focus on instructional leadership.

Written guidelines for safety exist in my school.
    I have no idea if written guidelines exist, but I talk about safety to all students.

I open the school building each morning.
    The custodian is responsible for opening and closing the school building.

I am precisely aware of how my building is utilized on a daily basis.
    I let my custodian and one of my APs discuss building utilization.

I believe that the physical aspects of the school plant and its maintenance contribute to overall school climate, which influences student achievement, albeit indirectly.
    I see no connection between the physical aspects of the school plant and student achievement.

I evaluate the effectiveness of main office procedures regularly.
    My secretary monitors all office stuff; I'm too busy.

I have a system in place to evaluate secretarial and clerical personnel.
    I have no system in place.

My office staff is familiar and conversant with the latest technologies.
    They don't even use e-mail.

I train all office staff on how to answer the phone and how to converse with visitors or school guests.
    I don't have to, because they usually do the right thing.

We have a master calendar posted in the main office.
    No master calendar exists.

I conduct regular meetings with all office staff.
    I have no time for such meetings.

All school records and important reports are kept confidential.
    I never thought about that.

I am familiar with basic budgetary procedures in my district.
    I'm clueless, but it doesn't affect my work in the school.

I oversee and evaluate food services in my school.
    I have no time to do so. They have their own supervisor.

I write clear memoranda.
    I write too many memoranda.

I use e-mail as an important method of communicating.
    I e-mail people too much, or so they tell me.

I have a copy of state codes of governance.
    I know of no such codes.

I understand the district budget cycle.
    I don't even know if one exists.

I oversee faculty and student books and instructional supply distribution.
    My secretary or AP does that.

I am aware of the varied furniture needs of my faculty.
    My secretary or AP handles that.

I know how to handle grievance hearings.
    I can't seem to keep up with all those regulations.

I have thoroughly read the district's Standard Operations Procedures Manual and keep it handy as a reference guide.
    Does one exist?

I provide training for staff regarding procedures to follow during health emergencies.
    I provide no such training.

My school has developed an emergency plan, and it is reviewed regularly.
    I have never developed such a plan, or I did develop one but have never enforced it.

Student accident reports are completed and filed appropriately and in a timely fashion.
    I rarely check if they are completed and filed properly.

I regularly evaluate school plant and facilities using either a formal evaluation form developed by the district or a self-developed form.
    I do not do so.

I am conversant with city or town health codes and can spot violations when they occur.
    I cannot.

I occasionally review collective bargaining agreements.
  I rarely do so.

In general, I manage time well.
  I am overwhelmed . . . ugh.

I can coordinate a schoolwide discipline plan.
  I delegate these duties to my APs.

I was fully prepared to coordinate lunch duty before I became a principal.
  I was not fully prepared to coordinate lunch duty before I became a principal.

I should be responsible for overseeing the school safety plan.
  Someone from the central office should, but not me, because I'm too busy.

It's always good to have taken course work to help prepare for management exigencies, even though we learn best on the job.
  All management issues can be learned on the job.

Reproducible #8. Meditations for Relaxation

Meditation Number 1: Progressive Muscle Relaxation

- Get into a comfortable position.
- Now take three deep breaths slowly, in through the nose and out through the mouth.
- Now take three more breaths, but this time very shallow breaths, in the same manner.
- Keep your eyes focused on staring forward.
- Take three deep slow breaths.
- Empty your mind of all thoughts. Do not think. Do not think about anything.
- Keep your eyes focused forward. Now take three slow shallow breaths.
- Now just stare for 10 seconds into space, breathing normally.
- As outside thoughts enter your mind, do not oppose them. Let them come, let them go. Keep your mind empty and eyes focused forward. If you must blink, then do so. Relax. Breathe normally. Be still. Try not to move. Stare for five more seconds.
- Now close your eyes gently. Breathe in through the nose and out through the mouth.
- Relax, relax, and relax.
- Now we are going to do something called progressive muscle relaxation.
- We are going to relax all the muscles in our body.
- First breathe normally and relax. Relax.
- Bend the toes of both feet very hard and keep them very tensed for five seconds—1, 2, 3, 4, 5.
- Release them, relax them, and breathe normally.
- Now tighten your ankles by bending your feet upward and hold for five seconds—1, 2, 3, 4, 5.
- Release them, and breathe.
- Now stiffen out your left leg only. Tense your leg muscles for five seconds—1, 2, 3, 4, 5.
- Release them, relax them, and breathe normally.
- Now stiffen out your right leg only. Tense your leg muscles for five seconds—1, 2, 3, 4, 5.
- Release them, relax them, and breathe.
- Now tighten your buttocks. Squeeze. Hold for five seconds—1, 2, 3, 4, 5.
- Release, relax, and breathe.
- Now tighten your stomach or abdominal muscles for five seconds—1, 2, 3, 4, 5.
- Release, relax, and breathe.
- Now pull both shoulders as far back as you can until your back muscles are very tense. Hold for five seconds—1, 2, 3, 4, 5.
- Release, relax, and breathe.
- Now make a fist with your left hand and squeeze for five seconds—1, 2, 3, 4, 5.
- Release, relax, and breathe.
- Now make a fist with your right hand and squeeze for five seconds—1, 2, 3, 4, 5.
- Release, relax, and breathe.
- Now clench your teeth. Squeeze your eyes shut very tightly and tense all your facial muscles and hold for five seconds—1, 2, 3, 4, 5.
- Release, relax, and breathe.
- Finally, tense your whole body—right now—1, 2, 3, 4, 5. Release, relax, and breathe.
- Take three deep breaths slowly, in through the nose and out through the mouth.
- Now take three more breaths, very shallow breaths, in the same way.
- You are now very, very relaxed— you are very relaxed.
- Just stay as you are and feel how vibrant and energized your body feels. Feel how relaxed you are.
- Slowly open your eyes and feel the relaxation.
- Breathe normally.
- You are perfectly relaxed, relaxed. You are now relaxed.

Meditation Number 2: Ratio Breathing

- Get into a comfortable position.
- Keep your eyes open. Let all thoughts come and go. Breathe naturally for now.
- Relax.
- Look around your surroundings.
- Breathe deeply now, in through your nose and out through your mouth.

    You are now ready for ratio breathing.

- Gently close your eyes.
- To a 3 count, breathe in through your nose; three slow, gentle breaths—1, 2, 3.
- Hold—1, 2, 3.
- Now exhale slowly through the mouth—1, 2, 3.
- Relax, relax.
- Breathe naturally now. Listen to your breathing. Notice how your diaphragm and chest expand as you inhale and collapse as you exhale. Breathe normally with your eyes still closed and relax.
- Relax.

    The ratio breathing exercise you have just completed was done to a 3-to-3 ratio count; that is, three breaths in and three breaths out. Now let's try it again.

- To a 3 count, breathe in through your nose; three slow, gentle breaths—1, 2, 3.
- Hold—1, 2, 3.
- Now exhale slowly—1, 2, 3.
- Breathe naturally now and listen to your breathing.

    Now let's try a 1-to-3 ratio breathing exercise.

- To a slow, gradual, one continuous count, breathe in all you can through your nose Now—1.
- Hold—1, 2, 3.
- Now slowly exhale—1, 2, 3.
- Be still. Try not to move.
- Relax, relax.

    Now let's try a 5-to-5 ratio count.

- To a very slow and gradual 5 count, breathe in five times—1, 2, 3, 4, 5.
- Hold—1, 2, 3, 4, 5.
- Now slowly exhale—1, 2, 3, 4, 5.
- Relax and breathe normally. Relax. Listen to your breathing.

    Now let's try a 1-to-1 ratio count.

- Breathe in evenly, yet quickly, through your nose to a 1 count. Ready—1.
- Hold—1, 2, 3.
- Exhale quickly and vigorously, now.
- Breathe normally and relax.
- Listen to your breathing pattern now.
- Relax. You are perfectly relaxed.
- You feel so relaxed, so relaxed. The only thing you are aware of is your quiet breathing. Relax.

Meditation Number 3: Guided Energy Breathing

- Stand up with your feet shoulder-width apart. Relax everything.
- Hands by your sides, head up, breathe normally. Relax.
- Gently close your eyes. Place your 10 fingertips touching at your tan-tien (2–3 inches below your navel).
- Feel your energy source. Feel the warmth generated by your fingertips touching your tan-tien.
- Your mind now sees the brilliant, shining light of energy; your fingertips feel it.
- Your body is relaxed, your mind is focused at the tan-tien.
- Let outside thoughts come and go. Do not oppose them. Just relax.
- As your fingertips are touching your tan-tien, it's very warm, very hot now—so energizing.
- Breathe normally and relax. Try not to move. Keep your eyes closed.
- Now clearly envision the bright shining light of energy in your mind, as you actually feel the energy with your fingertips.
- As your fingertips begin to move, very slowly upward toward your solar plexus in the middle of your chest, you can feel your energy light source following your fingertips, moving toward your solar plexus.
- Your fingertips have now reached the middle of your chest. You feel the warmth, the heat pulsating in your chest. It's a very good feeling, very energizing.
- Breathe deeply now, in through the nose and out through the mouth. Continue to breathe normally.
- Your mind is full of the vision of your bright energy source in the middle of your chest.
- It's pulsating, vibrating, alive.
- As your fingertips now begin to move very slowly upward, toward your forehead, you can feel the energy moving in your fingertips, moving toward your forehead.
- Your fingertips have now reached the middle of your forehead.
- You feel the warmth, the heat pulsating in your forehead.
- It feels so very good, so energizing.
- You feel the warmth of your energy in the middle of your forehead.
- Breathe naturally now.
- Relax.
- As your fingertips begin to move slowly down toward your tan-tien, you feel the energy moving along with your fingertips, past your chest, down toward the tan-tien.
- Your fingertips have now reached the tan-tien and are resting there gently.
- You feel the pulsating energy shining brightly in your mind.
- Breathe naturally.
- You feel so relaxed.
- Place your hands now by your sides and relax your body completely.
- Breathe naturally and gently, keep your eyes closed.
- Your mind and body are relaxed, energized.
- Your life/energy source is still as vibrant as ever.
- Your body and mind feel relaxed and energized.
- You're feeling great.
- Breathe.
- Relax, Relax.

Meditation Number 4: Hand Levitation

- Get into a comfortable position. Breathe naturally and relax.
- By directing your thoughts, you can make your hand feel as if it's rising easily, without effort.
- Keep your eyes closed and place your right arm straight out in front of you at shoulder height with the palm facing down.

- Now picture a garden hose with a strong stream of water pushing against the palm of your right hand, pushing against the palm of your hand.
- Think of a strong stream of water pushing your hand up. Let yourself feel the strong stream of water pushing up against the palm of your hand, pushing it up.
- Feel the force of the water pushing your hand up. Feel it pushing against the palm of your hand.
- Tell yourself that the force of the water is very strong; and as you think about it, let your hand begin to rise.
- Feel your hand rising, as you imagine a strong stream of water pushing it up and up, higher and higher.
- Tell yourself that a strong stream of water is pushing your hand up and up, raising your arm and hand higher and higher, as the strong stream of water just pushes it up.
- Higher and higher and higher.
- Now, tell yourself it's all in the mind and just let your hand and arm come back down slowly.
- Relax. Relax.
- Breathe deeply in through the nose and out through the mouth.
- Relax.

Meditation Number 5: Mind-Body Relaxation

- Breathe naturally. Get into a comfortable position.
- Keep your eyes closed.
- By letting your thoughts go along with these instructions, you can make your mind and body feel very relaxed.
- Picture yourself lying on the soft sand or on a beach towel that is soft and comfortable.
- Feel yourself lying on the soft sand or on a beach towel that is soft and comfortable.
- Let yourself feel the sun pleasantly warm, and feel the gentle breeze touching your neck and face.
- Picture the beautiful, clear blue sky, with fluffy little white clouds, drifting lazily by.
- Let yourself feel the soothing, penetrating warmth of the sun and tell yourself that your mind and body feel completely relaxed and perfectly at ease.
- Peaceful, relaxed, comfortable, calm, so at ease, at peace and totally relaxed, relaxed.
- Peaceful, relaxed, comfortable, calm, so at ease.
- Relaxed, relaxed, and relaxed.
- Peaceful, lazy, tranquil, calm, comfortable.
- Your mind and body are completely relaxed now, completely relaxed.

Part VII

Book Seven:
What Every Principal Should Know About Strategic Leadership

Overview of Strategic Leadership: Strengthen and Hone Your Strategic Leadership Skills for Effective School Planning

This is an essential guide for new and veteran school leaders focused on strategic planning, data-driven decision making, and transformational leadership. A comprehensive and practical handbook, it provides nine steps to strategic planning, plus guidelines for promoting a vision and mission, using data to empower and implement change, evaluating school programs, and moving from micropolitical to transformational leadership practice.

This last volume in a seven-part leadership series features examples and best practices, including:

- Insightful questionnaire and response analysis (TAKE THE SURVEY NOW on pages xiii–xiv.)
- Case study with reflective questions (READ THE CASE STUDY NOW and answer the reflective questions on pages 9–19.)
- "What You Should Know About" sections framing each chapter
- Self-assessment resources for leadership effectiveness
- "In-Basket Simulations" exploring real-life examples
- For leadership that can empower and transform a school community, this insightful volume provides a sure-footed path for leaders seeking to foster and manage effective and lasting change.

Best Practices in Planning Strategically

Overview

Research confirms that school leaders must remain "strategically intelligent" in order to manage and sustain the educational reform so vital to an organization (see, e.g., Davies & Davies, 2005). Change is an undeniable reality for any organization. Not all change means a school will be better off or that it will improve, but no improvement can occur without planned change. This chapter will introduce successful planning strategies, visioning, tips for conducting SWOT analyses, a sample guide to strategic planning, and one high school district's long-range plan. Systemic reform requires principals to exhibit strategic leadership skills. These principals strategize constantly and make strategic choices. We see that strategic leaders must have a thorough understanding of their schools. More specifically, this chapter covers:

- **Nine Steps to Successful Planning**—We review Mittenthal's (2002) nine steps for successful strategic planning.
- **Promoting Vision, Mission, and Goals**—We highlight some practical suggestions from Ramsey (2003) on vision making.
- **Conducting a SWOT Analysis**—Famous SWOT analysis is explained, in part, with information from the Alliance for Nonprofit Management (2003–2004).
- **A Guide to Strategic Planning**—Lyddon's (1999) 10 steps to strategic planning are detailed.
- **West Morris Regional High School District's (2000–2005) Long-Range Plan**—An example of a succinct plan is excerpted.

Discussion Questions

1. Why is strategic planning so important?

2. Do many principals you know engage in such planning? Explain why or why not.

3. How does a principal influence a strategic plan?

4. Who decides on the direction this plan will take?

5. What skills are necessary for those involved in the strategic planning process?

6. What steps might you suggest for successful strategic planning? (See Subsections 1 and 4.)

Engagement Activity

Time: 60–90 minutes

Materials: chart paper, markers, masking tape, *What Every Principal Should Know About Strategic Leadership* by Jeffrey Glanz

Refer to the "What You Should Know About Planning Strategically" section on pages 31–45. Divide the group into three groups by level: elementary, middle, and high school. Using the steps in Subsection 4 in the chapter, have each group work through as many steps as is feasible to develop a mock strategic plan. Have each group establish a context (type of school, makeup, personnel, resources, etc.) for their plan. If time remains, have the group critique the plan in Subsection 5. Post a piece of chart paper on a wall near where each group is meeting.

Have group members assign a recorder and a facilitator. After 40 minutes of group work, reconvene and have each group report out.

As a follow-up activity, have participants work through the questionnaire and accompanying material on pages xiii–lvi.

Best Practices in Data-Driven Decision Making

Overview

Effective principals use data to inform their curricular and instructional decisions school wide. In the "old" days, however, such data were limited to the yearly standardized test, usually given in late spring. Today, in the era of heightened accountability and, more important, in light of our deeper and more sophisticated notions of assessment (Popham, 2001), testing is varied and is considered only a part of the overall assessment system in place in a given school. Principals cull data from a variety of sources: standardized tests in various content areas, teacher-made tests, project-based learning activities, portfolios, surveys, and so forth. Long gone is the day when a principal made a decision in isolation of sufficient and rigorous data. It is commonly held today that "in a world of accountability, principals must be leaders in collecting and analyzing data to shape decisions that lead to continuous improvement" (Young, 2004, p. 96). Principals are now expected by school board members and region or district office administrative leaders to possess knowledge and skills in data analysis and interpretation as well as to use such data to inform decision making in order to best promote student achievement for all students. This chapter covers four topics related to data-driven decision making:

- **Learning From Role Models**—Exemplary practices of real principals are highlighted.
- **Using Data to Empower**—Shaver's (2004) guidelines for using data to make decisions are highlighted and expanded upon.
- **Collecting Data**—Primary and secondary ways of collecting data to inform your decision making are discussed.
- **Easy Steps to Program Evaluation**—Five steps you can use to evaluate programs are reviewed.

Discussion Questions

1. How do you use data to make decisions in your school?

2. What types of data do you use?

3. Do you use standardized test scores as the chief form of data? Why? If so, do you have any alternatives?

4. Which principals do you know who have used data to drive decision making effectively? What do they do so well? (See Subsection 1.)

5. Can you identify key guidelines for using data effectively? (See Subsection 2.)

6. What are the ways in which you collect data? (See Subsection 3.)

7. Have you ever undertaken a formal program evaluation? If so, describe the steps taken. (See Subsection 4.)

Engagement Activity

Time: 60–90 minutes

Materials: chart paper, markers, masking tape, *What Every Principal Should Know About Strategic Leadership* by Jeffrey Glanz

Refer to the "What You Should Know About Data-Driven Decision Making" section on pages 71–76. Divide the group into three groups by level: elementary, middle, and high school. Using the steps in Subsection 4 in the chapter, have each group work through as many steps as is feasible to evaluate a program. Have each group establish a context (type of school, program specifics, makeup, personnel, resources, etc.) for their plan. Post a piece of chart paper on a wall near where each group is meeting. Have group members assign a recorder and a facilitator. After 40 minutes of group work, reconvene and have each group report out.

As a follow-up activity, facilitate a discussion on how programs are developed and evaluated in the schools/districts of the participants.

Best Practices in Transformational Leadership

Overview

This chapter addresses the importance of transformational leadership in the strategic planning process. Arising in the 1980s, transformational leadership is aligned with attempts to change or transform individuals and the educational landscape as a whole. It combines both visionary and charismatic leadership approaches. Transforming schools is easy if done superficially. Such change, however, is ephemeral. This chapter highlights five areas all principals should consider about transformational leadership:

- **Understanding Micropolitical Leadership**—The political insights of Duffy (2003), Bolman and Deal (1997), and Ramsey (2003) are highlighted.
- **Understanding, Planning, and Implementing Change**—Robbins and Alvy's (2003) suggestions are summarized.
- **Monitoring Change**—Horsley and Loucks-Horsley's (1998) CBAM process is highlighted.
- **Leading Change**—Kaser and colleagues' (2002) actions for effective leadership are highlighted.
- **Becoming a Transformational Leader**—We review Marazza's (2003) five essentials of organizational excellence that can help transform your school.

Discussion Questions

1. Can you identify at least three different types of leadership?

2. Can you explain the difference between transactional and transformational leadership?

3. You know that politics is a very essential part of your job. How has politics played a key role in your position? What political challenges have you faced and are you currently facing?

4. Are you aware of what various theorists say about micropolitical leadership? (See Subsection 1.)

5. What advice might you offer a new principal on how to change teachers' attitudes about some instructional practices? (See suggestions in Subsection 2.)

6. Are you familiar with the CBAM process? (See Subsection 3.)

7. Have you ever seen transformational leadership in practice? If so, describe. (See Subsections 4 and 5.)

Engagement Activity

Time: 60 minutes

Materials: chart paper, markers, masking tape, *What Every Principal Should Know About Strategic Leadership* by Jeffrey Glanz

Refer to the "What You Should Know About Transformational Leadership" section on pages 78–104. Conduct a whole group discussion on how principals deal with change. Divide the group into four smaller groups. Post a piece of chart paper on a wall near where each group is meeting. Have group members assign a recorder and facilitator. First, have the group identify a real problem they face in school that requires a deep change approach. Have the group describe the challenge in detail. Before brainstorming possible approaches or solutions, have the group work through the chapter for five best ideas that might assist them in dealing with the problem or issue under discussion. Have the group then list and discuss ways they would deal with the issue. After 30 minutes of group work, reconvene and have each group report out.

As a follow-up activity, highlight the quotes in the chapter and have participants relate what each quote "says" to them.

Culminating Activity

Time: 60–90 minutes

Materials: This culminating activity utilizes Resources A and B in *What Every Principal Should Know About Strategic Leadership* by Jeffrey Glanz.

Divide the participants into two groups. One group will work on Resource A and the other group will work on Resource B. Make sure to provide copies of each Resource to each group (only one for each group, not one copy for each member because the group participation of all members will be enhanced by giving only one copy for the group). Allow groups to assign responsibilities to members:

Recorder—person responsible for recording info for group

Monitor—ensures that each group member participates (e.g., in the case of a silent member, the monitor might ask, "Steve, what do you think?" or "Do we all agree on the solution?")

Captain—ensures group stays on task to complete assigned task

Reporter—reports out to large group at end of session (may be one or two individuals)

What other roles/responsibilities can you encourage?

Resource A

Select as many in-basket simulations as time permits and brainstorm three specific strategies for coping/dealing with each scenario. Ensure all group members agree on each strategy (prioritize them here as relevant). During the report out phase, rather than just reading the scenario and reporting strategies, the group should first encourage audience reaction and participation and then share group strategies.

Resource B

Members administer the survey to the entire group. In other words, all session participants take the survey anonymously. Group members then tabulate results for a later presentation and discussion. Afterwards, Resource B group members offer their personal insights to questionnaire items. For instance, someone might share that she doesn't really feel comfortable giving workshops to teachers in a particular area. Discussion should occur within a collegial, non-threatening, and supportive environment encouraging alternate ways of seeing things and offering positive, constructive suggestions. Group members, during the reporting out session, should plan, in advance, key questions to provoke audience participation.

Strategic Leadership Reproducibles

Reproducible #1. Questionnaire

Directions: Using the following Likert scale, circle the answer that best represents your on-the-spot belief about each statement.

SA = Strongly Agree ("For the most part, yes.")
A = Agree ("Yes, but . . .")
D = Disagree ("No, but . . .")
SD = Strongly Disagree ("For the most part, no.")

SA   A   D   SD   1. I believe that long-term planning is important but impractical, because very few of us have the time.

SA   A   D   SD   2. There's no difference between long-term planning and strategic planning.

SA   A   D   SD   3. I see little, if any, connection between action research and strategic planning.

SA   A   D   SD   4. Data-driven decision making is a laborious process that is, in reality, quite simple and has marginal value at best because of the lack of a standard form of assessment.

SA   A   D   SD   5. I never let politics interfere with my work.

SA   A   D   SD   6. Strategic leaders realize that change is inevitable and therefore plan for it.

SA   A   D   SD   7. I am committed to social justice.

SA   A   D   SD   8. Building leadership capacity and sustainability are imperative for a strategic leader.

SA   A   D   SD   9. Transformational leadership is a principal's primary responsibility.

SA   A   D   SD   10. Learning about strategic planning would be facilitated by reading a sample Strategic Plan.

Reproducible #2. Strategic Leader Tasks

A strategic leader:

- Considers the present social, cultural, economic, and political realities that shape a school.
- Utilizes the unique talents of school faculty and staff to collaborate on planning initiatives.
- Sees and envisions future possibilities for nurturing, developing, and maintaining school excellence.
- Commits to visioning and possibilities for future growth and school improvement.
- Thinks creatively about different ways of improving his or her school.
- Conducts action research to generate ideas and to field-test possible solutions to problems.
- Involves many in-school and out-of-school officials in planning initiatives.
- Collects data to inform decision making.
- Is willing to change course if necessary based on newly accumulated data.
- Encourages innovative ideas and thinking by all members of the school community.
- Connects, in purposeful ways, strategic planning to promoting student achievement.

Reproducible #3. Quotations

Examine these quotations on strategic leadership. What do they mean to you?

"Thinking about and attempting to control the future are important components of planning."
—Henry Mintzberg

"One of the major differences between conventional planning and strategic planning is that conventional planning tends to be oriented toward looking at problems based on current understanding, or an inside-out mind set. Strategic planning requires an understanding of the nature of the issue, and then finding of an appropriate response, or an outside-in mind set."
—D. J. Rowley

"Critical is the realization that a school can engage in strategic planning—but lack strategy."
—Theodore Creighton

"The effective principal is like the quarterback of a football team. She pulls together a staff that is unified on where it is going and committed to the highest performance."
—James O'Hanlon and Donald O. Clifton

"Once the change has been identified, establish short- and long-term goals and corresponding strategies. Consider the following:

- *Who will be involved in making the change?*
- *Who will the change affect?*
- *How will those affected respond?"*
—Barbara L. Brock and Marilyn L. Grady

"Strategy . . . is something school leaders do before a problem arises."
—Theodore Creighton

"In the world of change leadership, every act is a political act."
—Francis M. Duffy

"[N]ot every plan is a strategic plan."
—Richard Mittenthal

"Whole-system change . . . requires educators to make sure their school districts create and maintain strategic alignment . . . to ensure that all the horses are pulling the wagon in the same direction."
—Francis M. Duffy

"If we want change to matter, to spread, and to last, then the system in which leaders do their work, must make sustainability a priority."
—Andy Hargreaves and Dean Fink

"A successful strategic planning process will examine and make informed projections about environmental realities to help an organization anticipate and respond to change by clarifying its mission and goals; targeting spending; and reshaping its programs."
—Richard Mittenthal

"The challenges are abundant, the responsibility awesome, and the need for moral leadership incalculable."
—Carolyn M. Shields

"Leading change in public education is tumultuous work. It is relentlessly intense, enormously complex, and often downright chaotic."

—Scott Thompson

"For strategic decision making to be effective, constraints and obstacles, as well as opportunities and challenges that impact the decision choice, must be identified."

—Petra E. Snowden and Richard A. Gorton

"I believe courageous, passionate, and visionary leaders . . . need to recognize that their effectiveness as change-leaders is the result of the skillful interplay of power, politics, and ethics."

—Francis M. Duffy

"Principals and other school leaders have been given a different charge: take an abundance of student data, mostly in the form of assessments, and turn this data into information to be used in improving educational practice."

—Jeffrey C. Wayman, Steve Midgley, and Sam Stringfield

"Strategic leaders are able to picture a range of possibilities several stages ahead of the current phase of organizational development."

—Jeff Jones

"Leading schools through complex reform agendas requires new leadership that goes far beyond improving test scores."

—Michael Fullan

"The principal's job is to design and nurture an environment in which teachers can more readily take charge of their work."

—Robert J. Starratt

"No matter how well long-range and strategic plans are developed and implemented, there are usually things that come up that necessitate more resources than most schools actually have."

—Elaine L. Wilmore

"Among the final steps toward institutional transformation, leaders will want to consolidate the improvements made, track and report on successes to stakeholders, and continue to inspire still more change."

—Robert C. Dickeson

"Optimal performance rests on the existence of a powerful shared vision that evolves through wide participation. . . . The test of greatness of a dream is that it has the energy to lift people out of their moribund ways to a level of being and relating from which the future can be faced with more hope."

—Robert Greenleaf

"Data cannot make decisions but decisions must be data-based."

—John H. Hansen and Elaine Liftin

"Evaluation involves not only looking at the outcomes or impact of a program but also documenting the process and progress of the program."

—Olatokunbo S. Fashola

"The leadership cadre at a school must pursue means to measure student achievement other than through standardized tests."

—John H. Hansen and Elaine Liftin

"If you want to determine if students can write, have them write something. If you want to determine if students can operate a machine, have them operate a machine. If you want to determine if students can conduct an experiment, have them conduct an experiment. In short, if you want to determine if they can perform a task, have them perform the task."

—Norman E. Gronlund

"The aim of assessment is primarily to educate and improve student performance, not merely to audit it."

—Grant Wiggins

"Leadership is one of the most observed and least understood phenomena on earth."

—James MacGregor Burns

"Rather than being a model that tells leaders what to do, transformational leadership provides a broad set of generalizations of what is typical of leaders who are transforming contexts."

—Peter G. Northouse

"To exercise leadership in this climate of change will require deep convictions, strong commitments, and clear ideas about directions for changes in the form and content of schooling."

—Robert J. Starratt

Reproducible #4. Program Evaluation in Five Steps

I. Focusing the Evaluation is composed of three steps:

1. Clarify evaluation purposes.

2. Clarify what is to be evaluated.

3. Identify questions to be answered.

II. Collecting Data is done via the following methods: teacher and pupil interviews, teacher-made tests, and checklists for completed assignments.

III. Organizing and Analyzing the Data

IV. Reporting the Data

V. Administering the Evaluation

Reproducible #5. Realities of Strategic Leadership: In-Basket Simulations

During an interview, you are asked to respond to the following scenarios or questions:

• You are the newly assigned principal of an urban high school in which strategic planning has never been adopted. You intend to develop such a plan. Describe the steps you would take to initiate, implement, and monitor the plan.

• As a new principal in a suburban middle school, you share your vision for inclusive practice to the faculty. Most faculty members are tenured, with an average of 14 years' teaching experience. You find few volunteers for your goal-setting committee. You surmise that teachers are resisting your emphasis on inclusion. One teacher tells you point-blank, "We don't want special education kids included in our classes full time. We have enough classroom-management problems without having to add these other 'needy' kids." How do you react to such resistance to your ideas?

• You cannot find any volunteers to join the action research committee designed to undertake a needs assessment that will form the basis for your strategic plan. What do you do?

• As elementary school principal in a suburban neighborhood with limited financial and material resources, you find that you must prioritize the numerous proposals requesting funds. You decide to fund the school trip committee's proposal but turn down the request from the textbook committee. Jim, a tenured faculty member who chairs the committee, demands an explanation of why his proposal was rejected. Before letting you respond, he states emphatically, "If my committee's proposal is not funded, the fifth-grade teachers will no longer participate in the strategic plan initiative." Your response?

• Would you write the strategic plan by yourself? Explain why or why not.

• As a high school principal, you inform the English department that according to data collected over the past semester, students are not making adequate progress academically. You request a plan from the department to raise student achievement. The department chairperson responds to your request by claiming that the data used were erroneous. "In fact," he says, "according to our internal data, students are performing quite well." How would you respond?

• As a brand-new principal, during your first day on the job in an urban high school, you are challenged by the fact that the school has a long history of inadequate leadership (six principals over a three-year period) and a faculty whose members quarrel frequently, rarely socialize with each other, and contend with each other for scarce resources. You want to undertake a SWOT analysis and then act on a strategic plan to help mend wounds and rally faculty around a common vision and mission. Describe your actions in detail. How do politics affect your work, and how would you overcome your political challenges?

• Your middle school is riddled with high teacher turnover, partly because the school is located in a low-socioeconomic-status part of town. Over 95% of students in your school receive free lunch. Teachers work in isolation of each other and rarely, if ever, meet to discuss instructional or curricular issues. Your two assistant principals don't like each other and are not very hard workers. You surmise that they are burned out. Parent involvement is negligible, and teacher and staff morale is low. You want to transform this school into a model school for the district and even the state. You are highly energetic and enthusiastic. As a people-oriented leader and being new to the school (recently transferred from another school in the district), you know much about transformational leadership. How would you go about building leadership capacity and sustainability in this school? Describe your actions in detail.

• You are the newly assigned principal of an elementary school, and you are interested in undertaking a needs assessment. You want to survey how staff, parents, and students feel about the effectiveness of the school's goals in three areas: curriculum, organization, and school climate. Your questionnaire should include items about academic goals, monitoring of student progress, teacher effectiveness, administrative leadership, rewards and incentives for students, order and discipline, parent and community involvement, and so forth. Describe how you would use these results to improve your school, paying particular attention to student achievement.

• You have implemented a new literacy-based reading program in your middle school. How would you go about assessing its effectiveness?

• You want to transform your school, but "politics" seems to be getting in the way. Identify three primary political obstacles and how you would go about dealing with them in order to effectively pursue your goal of transformational leadership.

• What are the connections among strategic planning, data-driven decision making, and transformational leadership?

Reproducible #6. Assessing Your Role in Strategic Leadership

SA = Strongly Agree ("For the most part, yes.")
A = Agree ("Yes, but . . .")
D = Disagree ("No, but . . .")
SD = Strongly Disagree ("For the most part, no.")

SA A D SD 1. I believe that strategic planning is well worth the effort and time it takes.

SA A D SD 2. I possess the knowledge necessary to implement a strategic plan.

SA A D SD 3. A well-designed strategic plan can make a big difference in my effectiveness as principal.

SA A D SD 4. I am committed to following through on my school's strategic plan.

SA A D SD 5. I will allocate sufficient funds to ensure that strategic goals are achieved.

SA A D SD 6. I am the most critical element that determines success of the strategic plan.

SA A D SD 7. My faculty and district colleagues support my vision of excellence for all students.

SA A D SD 8. Strategic planning is only as important as the goal of promoting high achievement for all students.

SA A D SD 9. I solicit input from internal and external stakeholders for my school's strategic plan.

SA A D SD 10. I would solicit assistance of outside consultants to help frame the strategic plan.

SA A D SD 11. I can articulate the relationship between strategic planning and high student achievement.

SA A D SD 12. I revisit the strategic plan on a yearly basis.

SA A D SD 13. The process of strategic planning is more important than the plan itself.

SA A D SD 14. There's no one best plan—I continually reflect, discuss, and revise portions of the plan to meet current and future needs.

SA A D SD 15. Strategic planning is an incremental, gradual process that does not provide panaceas for the work we do in schools.

SA   A   D   SD   16. I see my role as advocate and facilitator in the strategic planning process.

SA   A   D   SD   17. I discuss the strategic plan constantly in various forums and meetings.

SA   A   D   SD   18. Teacher involvement and leadership are critical to the plan's success.

SA   A   D   SD   19. I continually consult with my superintendent for support and input related to the school's strategic plan.

SA   A   D   SD   20. I invite suggestions and constructive criticisms at all phases in the strategic planning process.

SA   A   D   SD   21. Beyond the initial stages, the principal need not be directly involved in the strategic planning process, as long as someone is designated to be in charge.

SA   A   D   SD   22. Effective strategic leaders encourage everyone in the school building to participate in the strategic planning process.

SA   A   D   SD   23. Division of responsibilities for carrying out the strategic plan should be open, flexible, and on a volunteer basis, without designating or identifying specific individuals to take responsibility for certain areas.

SA   A   D   SD   24. There's no need to involve school board members in the strategic planning process.

SA   A   D   SD   25. Strategic planning committees should always meet often.

SA   A   D   SD   26. Establishing specific timelines is inadvisable because it is so restrictive.

SA   A   D   SD   27. The strategic planning process should be monitored by anyone who shows interest in doing so.

SA   A   D   SD   28. Strategic planning is likely to be short term.

SA   A   D   SD   29. I try to minimize politics in the strategic planning process.

SA   A   D   SD   30. As strategic leader, I will take any action to ensure success.

Sample Workshop Agendas

Half-Day Workshop Agendas

Theme   A half-day workshop can be conducted on any one of the seven leadership approaches: instructional, cultural, ethical/spiritual, collaborative, school-community, operational, or strategic.

Seven half-day formats are presented here (one for each leadership approach). Primary material is a copy of the volume for each participant.

Feel free to use one of the starter activities discussed in the Introduction: Discussion Questions, K-W-L Activity, and/or Interview Questions.

INSTRUCTIONAL LEADERSHIP

Introductory Activity (25 minutes)

- Administer Questionnaire on pages xiii–xiv.
- Read prefatory information on pages xv–xvi. Use Reflective Questions on page xvi as a guide to discussion.
- Review responses to each question on questionnaire. See suggested responses on pages xviii–xx. Facilitator can either read answers or call upon participants. Use Reflective Questions on page xx.
- Using PowerPoint slides, Reproducibles, or taken directly from the book (pages xvii–xviii), examine each of the quotes and their meaning for participants—this sets the tone for the workshop.

Purpose of Workshop (5 minutes)

- Highlight the importance of instructional leadership as critical to the success of a principal.
- Understand how supervision and professional development are critical to instructional leadership.
- Implement a complete clinical supervision cycle.
- Reflect on supervision and instructional leadership.

Chapter 4: (pages 56–72) [2 hours]

1. Set tone for the clinical supervision cycle. (Read pages 56–59.)

2. Discuss the three approaches used for individuals of varying levels of experience (pages 59–65). Role-play in triads with one person playing the role of observer. Show video excerpts from "Supervision in Practice" videotape. (Contact Corwin Press for details.)

3. Work through each of the three steps of clinical supervision (pages 65–72).

For further detail, see *Supervision That Improves Teaching* by Corwin Press.
Case Study (pages 8–11) [30 minutes], use Reflective Questions (page 11) as guide.
Summary and Evaluation (15 minutes)

* * * * * * * * * *

CULTURAL LEADERSHIP

Introductory Activity (25 minutes)

- Administer Questionnaire on pages xiii–xv.
- Read prefatory information on page xvi. Use Reflective Questions on page xvii as a guide to discussion.
- Review responses to each question on questionnaire. See suggested responses on pages xviii–xxiv. Facilitator can either read answers or call upon participants. Use Reflective Questions on page xxiv.
- Using PowerPoint slides, Reproducibles, or taken directly from the book (pages xvii–xviii), examine each of the quotes and their meaning for participants—this sets the tone for the workshop.

Purpose of Workshop (5 minutes)

- Highlight the importance of cultural leadership as critical to the success of a principal.
- Understand how a vision statement is formulated and why it's critical to cultural leadership.
- Develop a draft vision statement.
- Reflect on visioning and cultural leadership.

Chapter 4: (pages 33–50) [2 hours]

1. Set tone for vision statement development. (Read pages 33–35.)

2. Work through pages 36–40 (examining beliefs and values), using Reflective Questions as appropriate. Participants may want to work in pairs on this activity, although personal information articulated may be sensitive and some participants may want to keep their ideas private.

3. Compose a first draft of a vision statement using pages 41–47 as a guide, along with sample vision statement. Note that product produced by participants can be much briefer than sample provided.

4. Discuss how to actualize one's vision by using pages 47–48 as a guide.

5. If time permits, work through case provided on pages 48–50, along with Reflective Questions on page 50.

   For further detail, see Chapter 4 in *Building Effective Learning Communities* (Corwin Press).
   Case Study (pages 13–16) [30 minutes], use Reflective Questions (page 16) as guide.
   Summary and Evaluation (15 minutes)

* * * * * * * * * *

ETHICAL/SPIRITUAL LEADERSHIP

Introductory Activity (25 minutes)

- Administer Questionnaire on pages xiii–xv.
- Read prefatory information on page xvi. Use Reflective Questions on page xviii as a guide to discussion.
- Review responses to each question on questionnaire. See suggested responses on pages xix–xxvi. Facilitator can either read answers or call upon participants. Use Reflective Questions on page xxvi.
- Using PowerPoint slides, Reproducibles, or taken directly from the book (pages xviii–xix and pages 11–13), examine each of the quotes and their meaning for participants—this sets the tone for the workshop.

Purpose of Workshop (5 minutes)

- Highlight the import of ethical and spiritual leadership as critical to the success of a principal.
- Explore the differences and similarities among ethical, moral, and spiritual awareness.
- Assess one's own proclivity to ethical, moral, and spiritual behavior.
- Reflect on the moral imperatives of leading.

Chapters 2 & 3: (pages 17–52) [2 hours]

1. Using the material on the Web site that accompanies this book, have participants take the questionnaire on leadership virtues or excellences. Follow directions, and facilitate discussion.

2. Use the Reflective Questions to summarize or highlight main points.

   For further detail, see *Finding Your Leadership Style* by the Association for Supervision and Curriculum Development (ASCD).

3. Using material in the Conclusion (pages 62–68), lead discussion of what the moral imperatives of the school principalship are.

   Case Study (pages 14–16) [30 minutes], use Reflective Questions (page 16) as guide.
   Summary and Evaluation (15 minutes)

* * * * * * * * * *

COLLABORATIVE LEADERSHIP

Introductory Activity (25 minutes)

- Administer Questionnaire on pages xiii–xv.
- Read prefatory information on pages xvi–xvii. Use Reflective Questions on page xvii as a guide to discussion.
- Review responses to each question on questionnaire. See suggested responses on pages xix–xxvi. Facilitator can either read answers or call upon participants. Use Reflective Questions on page xxvi.
- Using PowerPoint slides, Reproducibles, or taken directly from the book (pages xviii–xix and pages 10–11), examine each of the quotes and their meaning for participants—this sets the tone for the workshop.

Purpose of Workshop (5 minutes)

- Highlight the importance of collaborative leadership as critical to the success of a principal.
- Understand how important team building is to collaborative leadership.
- Appreciate the Importance of self-knowledge in team building.
- Understand how to build effective teams.

Chapter 2: (pages 16–50) [2 hours]

1. Set tone for team building by reviewing advantages of teaming (pages 18–19).

2. Review characteristics of effective teams (pages 22–25).

3. Using the PowerPoint presentation as a guide, lead participants in an assessment of their leadership styles. The premise is based on the notion that self-knowledge is a prerequisite for team building. Participants spend 20 minutes taking survey (pages 29–33), followed by highlights of seven leadership qualities. Implications discussion follows.

4. Review Chapter Subsections 4 and 5 for team development and assessment.

For further detail, see *Finding Your Leadership Style* by the Association for Supervision and Curriculum Development (ASCD).

Case Study (pages 12–15) [30 minutes], use Reflective Questions (page 15) as guide.
Summary and Evaluation (15 minutes)

* * * * * * * * * *

SCHOOL-COMMUNITY LEADERSHIP

Introductory Activity (25 minutes)

- Administer Questionnaire on pages xiii–xv.
- Read prefatory information on page xvi. Use Reflective Questions on page xvii as a guide to discussion.
- Review responses to each question on questionnaire. See suggested responses on pages xviii–xxviii. Facilitator can either read answers or call upon participants. Use Reflective Questions on pages xxviii–xxix.
- Using PowerPoint slides, Reproducibles, or taken directly from the book (pages xvii–xviii and pages 10–11), examine each of the quotes and their meaning for participants—this sets the tone for the workshop.

Purpose of Workshop (5 minutes)

- Highlight the importance of school-community leadership as critical to the success of a principal.
- Understand best practices for reaching out to parents and why it's critical to school-community leadership.
- Develop a systematic plan to involve parents.
- Reflect on school-community leadership.

Chapters 2 & 3: (pages 15–63) [2 hours]

1. Using chapter quotes and prefatory information on PowerPoint, present an overview to participants, thus setting a tone for the workshop.

2. Divide group into at least two smaller groups and assign a chapter to each group. Using markers and posted paper, have group identify all the practical strategies for soliciting parental and community involvement, respectively. Report out as usual at the end.

3. Reflect on school-community leadership using Conclusion material on pages 75–76.

Case Study (pages 12–14) [30 minutes], use Reflective Questions (page 14) as guide.
Summary and Evaluation (15 minutes)

* * * * * * * * * *

OPERATIONAL LEADERSHIP

Introductory Activity (25 minutes)

- Administer Questionnaire on pages xiii–xv.
- Read prefatory information on page xvi–xvii. Use Reflective Questions on page xvi–xvii as a guide to discussion.
- Review responses to each question on questionnaire. See suggested responses on pages xviii–xxxiii. Facilitator can either read answers or call upon participants. Use Reflective Questions on page xxxiii.
- Using PowerPoint slides, Reproducibles, or taken directly from the book (pages xvii–xviii and pages 7–8), examine each of the quotes and their meaning for participants—this sets the tone for the workshop.

Purpose of Workshop (5 minutes)

- Highlight the importance of operational leadership as critical to the success of a principal.
- Understand and develop skills in organization, facilities management, budgeting, human resources management, communication, and personal renewal.
- Reflect on operational leadership.

Chapters 2–7: (pages 15–125) [2 hours]

1. Using Figure 1.1 on page 5 set a tone for the workshop.

2. Divide group into six groups and have them select a chapter to review (match by interest, keeping group numbers fairly even). Using markers and posted paper, have each group identify all the practical strategies related to their chapter. Report out as usual at the end and follow each chapter with discussion.

3. Reflect on operational leadership using Conclusion material on pages 126–128.

Case Study (pages 8–13) [30 minutes], use Reflective Questions (page 13) as guide.
Summary and Evaluation (15 minutes)

* * * * * * * * * *

STRATEGIC LEADERSHIP

Introductory Activity (25 minutes)

- Administer Questionnaire on pages xiii–xiv.
- Read prefatory information on page xv. Use Reflective Questions on page xvi as a guide to discussion.
- Review responses to each question on questionnaire. See suggested responses on pages xvii–lv. Facilitator can either read answers or call upon participants. Use Reflective Questions on pages lv–lvi.
- Using PowerPoint slides, Reproducibles, or taken directly from the book (pages xvi–xvii), examine each of the quotes and their meaning for participants—this sets the tone for the workshop.

Purpose of Workshop (5 minutes)

- Highlight the import of strategic leadership as critical to the success of a principal.
- Understand how to plan strategically.
- Implement a program evaluation.
- Reflect on strategic leadership.

Chapters 2 & 3: (pages 20–77) [2 hours]

1. Using chapter quotes and prefatory information on PowerPoint, present an overview to participants, thus setting a tone for the workshop.

2. Divide group into at least two smaller groups and assign a chapter to each group. Using markers and posted paper, have each group identify all the practical strategies for planning strategically and making decisions with data, respectively. Report out as usual at the end.

3. Reflect on strategic leadership using Conclusion material on pages 105–106.

4. **After lunch:** Using pages 71–76, guide participants in program evaluation (use PowerPoint to facilitate). Divide into groups and have teams develop a mock program and evaluation. Report out at end.

Case Study (pages 9–19) [30 minutes], use Reflective Questions (page 19) as a guide.
Summary and Evaluation (15 minutes)

For further detail, see Chapter 4 in *Building Effective Learning Communities* by Corwin Press.
Case Study (pages 13–16) [30 minutes], use Reflective Questions (page 16) as guide.
Summary and Evaluation (15 minutes)

One-Day Workshop Agendas

Theme A one-day workshop can be conducted on any one of the seven leadership approaches: instructional, cultural, ethical/spiritual, collaborative, school-community, operational, or strategic.

Seven one-day formats are presented here (one for each leadership approach). Primary material is a copy of the volume for each participant.

A format is also included for a one-day workshop on all seven forms of leadership. Obviously, one cannot go into much depth for each, but participants can explore the day-to-day realities of leading with all seven forms in mind.

Feel free to use one of the starter activities discussed in the Introduction: Discussion Questions, K-W-L Activity, and/or Interview Questions.

INSTRUCTIONAL LEADERSHIP

Introductory Activity (25 minutes)

- Administer Questionnaire on pages xiii–xiv.
- Read prefatory information on pages xv–xvi. Use Reflective Questions on page xvi as a guide to discussion.
- Review responses to each question on questionnaire. See suggested responses on pages xviii–xx. Facilitator can either read answers or call upon participants. Use Reflective Questions on page xx.
- Using PowerPoint slides, Reproducibles, or taken directly from the book (pages xvii–xviii), examine each of the quotes and their meaning for participants—this sets the tone for the workshop.

Purpose of Workshop (5 minutes)

- Highlight the importance of instructional leadership as critical to the success of a principal.
- Understand how supervision and professional development are critical to instructional leadership.
- Implement a complete clinical supervision cycle.
- Reflect on supervision and instructional leadership.
- Use action research as instructional improvement.

Chapter 4: (pages 56–72) [2 hours]

1. Set tone for the clinical supervision cycle. (Read pages 56–59.)

2. Discuss the three approaches used for individuals of varying levels of experience (pages 59–65). Role-play in triads with one person playing role of observer. Show video excerpts from "Supervision in Practice" videotape. (Contact Corwin Press for details.)

3. Work through each of the three steps of clinical supervision (pages 65–72).

For further detail, see *Supervision That Improves Teaching* (Corwin Press).
Case Study (pages 8–11) [30 minutes], use Reflective Questions (page 11) as guide.

Lunch Break
Afternoon Session
Chapter 4 and selected portions, at facilitator's discretion, of Chapter 2: (pages 72–83)
[3 hours]

1. Compose a PowerPoint presentation as a guide.

2. Review the importance of action research as a new form of supervision.

3. Discuss case studies on pages 73–78, divide groups into two.

4. Facilitate groups to develop action research strategies for principal leadership development or as a means of encouraging teacher action research.

5. Use action research video published by the Association for Supervision and Curriculum Development (ASCD).

6. Integrate various teaching ideas from Chapter 2.

7. Review suggestions for principals (pages 79–83).
   Summary and Evaluation (15 minutes)

* * * * * * * * * *

CULTURAL LEADERSHIP

Introductory Activity (25 minutes)

- Administer Questionnaire on pages xiii–xv.
- Read prefatory information on page xvi. Use Reflective Questions on page xvii as a guide to discussion.
- Review responses to each question on questionnaire. See suggested responses on pages xviii–xxiv. Facilitator can either read answers or call upon participants. Use Reflective Questions on page xxiv.
- Using PowerPoint slides, Reproducibles, or taken directly from the book (pages xvii–xviii), examine each of the quotes and their meaning for participants—this sets the tone for the workshop.

Purpose of Workshop (5 minutes)

- Highlight the importance of cultural leadership as critical to the success of a principal.
- Understand how a vision statement is formulated and why it's critical to cultural leadership.
- Develop a draft vision statement.
- Understanding change and renewal in the school organization.
- Reflect on visioning and cultural leadership.

Chapter 4: (pages 33–50) [2 hours]

1. Set tone for vision statement development. (Read pages 33–35.)

2. Work through pages 36–40 (examining beliefs and values) using Reflective Questions as appropriate. Participants may want to work in pairs on this activity, although personal information articulated may be sensitive and some participants may want to keep their ideas private.

3. Compose a first draft of a vision statement using pages 41–47 as a guide, along with sample vision statement. Note that product produced by participants can be much briefer than sample provided.

4. Discuss how to actualize one's vision by using pages 47–48 as a guide.

5. If time permits, work through case provided on pages 48–50, along with Reflective Questions on page 50.

For further detail, see Chapter 4 in *Building Effective Learning Communities* by Corwin Press.

Lunch Break
Afternoon Session
Chapter 5: (pages 67–83) [2–3 hours]

1. Using Figure 5.1, lead a discussion on the various external and internal influences on the school organization. Address these two questions for starters:
    *   How do societal/historical/economic/political factors influence the school and your role as principal?
    *   How do you stimulate school renewal toward higher levels of achievement?

2. Use the following case as a means to spark discussion about cultural diversity and change (change in people's attitudes):

    You are principal of a middle school in a neighborhood that has had a marked increase of African American students. Neighborhood demographics have changed dramatically from an all white student body to nearly 35% black, with many white, middle-class families moving out of the neighborhood. The staff is primarily white and many teachers are complaining about the lack of parental involvement, increase in misbehavior and serious behavioral issues, and a decline on test scores in reading and math as measured by in-class teacher-developed examinations. Faculty representatives report that they are dissatisfied with the school's academic programming and low achievement of students, particularly among the African American students.
    *   What societal/historical/economic/political factors are at play here?
    *   What other personal or interpersonal factors may influence teachers' perceptions of the academic abilities of African American students?
    *   How do you as principal address the teachers' concerns?
    *   How do you address the negative climate pervasive in the school?
    *   What cultural shifts are needed to best address the issues raised in the case?
        Divide into groups for discussion and reporting out at the end. Encourage workshop participants to use chapter content to address the case.

3. How do the suggestions on pages 80–83 help to address school renewal as related in particular to the previous case, and to your school in general?

4. Using Figure 6.1, have participants discuss how each of the domains can lead to a renewed and reinvigorated school culture.

    Case Study (pages 13–16) [30 minutes], use Reflective Questions (page 16) as guide.
    Summary and Evaluation (15 minutes)

* * * * * * * * * *

ETHICAL/SPIRITUAL LEADERSHIP

Introductory Activity (25 minutes)

*   Administer Questionnaire on pages xiii–xv.
*   Read prefatory information on page xvi. Use Reflective Questions on page xviii as a guide to discussion.
*   Review responses to each question on questionnaire. See suggested responses on pages xix–xxvi. Facilitator can either read answers or call upon participants. Use Reflective Questions on page xxvi.
*   Using PowerPoint slides, Reproducibles, or taken directly from the book (pages xviii–xix and pages 11–13), examine each of the quotes and their meaning for participants—this sets the tone for the workshop.

Purpose of Workshop (5 minutes)

*   Highlight the importance of ethical and spiritual leadership as critical to the success of a principal.

- Explore the differences and similarities among ethical, moral, and spiritual awareness.
- Assess one's own proclivity to ethical, moral, and spiritual behavior.
- Work through ethical dilemmas.
- Reflect on the moral imperatives of leading.

Chapters 2 & 3: (pages 17–52) [2 hours]

1. Using the material on the Web site that accompanies this book, have participants take the questionnaire on leadership virtues or excellences. Follow directions and facilitate discussion.

2. Use the Reflective Questions to summarize or highlight main points
      For further detail, see *Finding Your Leadership Style* by the Association for Supervision and Curriculum Development (ASCD).

3. Using material in the Conclusion (pages 62–68), lead discussion of what the moral imperatives of the school principalship are.

Lunch Break
Afternoon Session
Chapter 4: (pages 53–61) [2–3 hours]

1. Using the material in the chapter, highlight various approaches and ways to help principals react to the various ethical dilemmas they encounter.

2. Brainstorm various ethical dilemmas principals may face.

3. Break into groups for detailed discussion, followed by reporting out and whole group overview.

4. Use ethical dilemmas on pages 70–72 to provoke thought and discussion.

Case Study (pages 14–16) [30 minutes], use Reflective Questions (page 16) as guide.
Summary and Evaluation (15 minutes)

* * * * * * * * * *

COLLABORATIVE LEADERSHIP

Introductory Activity (25 minutes)

- Administer Questionnaire on pages xiii–xv.
- Read prefatory information on page xvi–xvii. Use Reflective Questions on page xvii as a guide to discussion.
- Review responses to each question on questionnaire. See suggested responses on pages xix–xxvi. Facilitator can either read answers or call upon participants. Use Reflective Questions on page xxvi.
- Using PowerPoint slides, Reproducibles, or taken directly from the book (pages xviii–xix and pages 10–11), examine each of the quotes and their meaning for participants—this sets the tone for the workshop.

Purpose of Workshop (5 minutes)

- Highlight the importance of collaborative leadership as critical to the success of a principal.
- Understand how important team building is to collaborative leadership.
- Appreciate the importance of self-knowledge in team building.
- Understand how to build effective teams.
- Use action research for collaboration.

Chapter 2: (pages 16–50) [2 hours]

1. Set tone for team building by reviewing advantages of teaming (pages 18–19).

2. Review characteristics of effective teams (pages 22–25).

3. Using a PowerPoint presentation as a guide, lead participants in an assessment of their leadership styles. The premise is based on the notion that self-knowledge is a prerequisite for team building. Participants spend 20 minutes taking survey (pages 29–33), followed by highlights of seven leadership qualities. Implications discussion follows.

4. Review Chapter Subsections 4 and 5 for team development and assessment.

For further detail, see *Finding Your Leadership Style* by the Association for Supervision and Curriculum Development (ASCD).

Lunch Break
Afternoon Session
Chapter 3: (pages 51–69) [2–3 hours]

1. Use PowerPoint on action research to guide material in chapter.

2. Allow groups to design collaborative efforts through action research projects.

Case Study (pages 12–15) [30 minutes], use Reflective Questions (page 15) as guide.
Summary and Evaluation (15 minutes)

* * * * * * * * * *

SCHOOL-COMMUNITY LEADERSHIP

Introductory Activity (25 minutes)

- Administer Questionnaire on pages xiii–xv.
- Read prefatory information on page xvi. Use Reflective Questions on page xvii as a guide to discussion.
- Review responses to each question on questionnaire. See suggested responses on pages xviii–xxviii. Facilitator can either read answers or call upon participants. Use Reflective Questions on pages xxviii–xxix.
- Using PowerPoint slides, Reproducibles, or taken directly from the book (pages xvii–xviii and pages 10–11), examine each of the quotes and their meaning for participants—this sets the tone for the workshop.

Purpose of Workshop (5 minutes)

- Highlight the importance of school-community leadership as critical to the success of a principal.
- Understand best practices for reaching out to parents and why it's critical to school-community leadership.
- Develop a systematic plan to involve parents.
- Understand and take proactive steps to address black–white achievement gap.
- Reflect on school-community leadership.

Chapters 2, 3, & 4: (pages 15–63) [2–4 hours]

1. Using chapter quotes and prefatory information on PowerPoint, present an overview to participants, thus setting a tone for the workshop.

2. Divide group into at least two smaller groups and assign a chapter to each group. Using markers and posted paper, have each group identify all the practical strategies for soliciting parental and community involvement, respectively. Report out as usual at the end.

3. **After lunch:** Using the material in Chapter 4 (pages 64–74), conduct a whole group discussion on closing the black–white achievement gap, stressing practical strategies. Make certain you are acquainted with this topic as parts of the discussion may be controversial. How would you respond to someone who said, "There's no such thing. . . ." etc.? Refer to Rothstein's (2004) monumental and very useful book, *Class and Schools: Using Social, Economic, and Educational Reform to Close the Black-White Achievement Gap.*

4. Reflect on school-community leadership using Conclusion material on pages 75–76.

    Case Study (pages 12–14) [30 minutes], use Reflective Questions (page 14) as guide.

    Summary and Evaluation (15 minutes)

* * * * * * * * * *

OPERATIONAL LEADERSHIP

Introductory Activity (25 minutes)

*   Administer Questionnaire on pages xiii–xv.
*   Read prefatory information on pages xvi–xvii. Use Reflective Questions on pages xvi–xvii as a guide to discussion.
*   Review responses to each question on questionnaire. See suggested responses on pages xviii–xxxiii. Facilitator can either read answers or call upon participants. Use Reflective Questions on page xxxiii.
*   Using PowerPoint slides, Reproducibles, or taken directly from the book (pages xvii–xviii and pages 7–8), examine each of the quotes and their meaning for participants—this sets the tone for the workshop.
    Purpose of Workshop (5 minutes)
*   Highlight the importance of operational leadership as critical to the success of a principal.
*   Understand and develop skills in organization, facilities management, budgeting, human resources management, communication, and personal renewal.
*   Reflect on operational leadership.

    Chapters 2–7 (pages 15–125) [3–4 hours]—The following content is not different from that covered in the half-day agenda, but a full-day facilitator can address some content before lunch, or go into one or two areas in more depth in the afternoon (e.g., personal renewal with relaxation exercises, etc.).

1. Use Figure 1.1 on page 5 to set a tone for the workshop.

2. Divide group into six groups and have them select a chapter to review (match by interest, keeping group numbers fairly even). Using markers and posted paper, have each group identify all the practical strategies related to their chapter. Report out as usual at the end and follow each chapter with a discussion.

3. Reflect on operational leadership using Conclusion material on pages 126–128.

    Case Study (pages 8–13) [30 minutes], use Reflective Questions (page 13) as guide.
    Summary and Evaluation (15 minutes)

* * * * * * * * * *

STRATEGIC LEADERSHIP

Introductory Activity (25 minutes)

- Administer Questionnaire on pages xiii–xiv.
- Read prefatory information on page xv–xvi. Use Reflective Questions on page xvi as a guide to discussion.
- Review responses to each question on questionnaire. See suggested responses on pages xvii–lvi. Facilitator can either read answers or call upon participants. Use Reflective Questions on page xxiv.
- Using PowerPoint slides, Reproducibles, or taken directly from the book (pages xvi–xvii and pages 8–9), examine each of the quotes and their meaning for participants—this sets the tone for the workshop.

Purpose of Workshop (5 minutes)

- Highlight the import of strategic leadership as critical to the success of a principal.
- Understand how to plan strategically.
- Implement a program evaluation.
- Reflect on strategic leadership.

Chapters 2 & 3: (pages 20–77) [2 hours]

1. Using chapter quotes and prefatory information on PowerPoint, present an overview to participants, thus setting a tone for the workshop.

2. Divide group into at least two smaller groups and assign a chapter to each group. Using markers and posted paper, have each group identify all the practical strategies for planning strategically and making decisions with data, respectively. Report out as usual at the end.

3. Reflect on strategic leadership using Conclusion material on pages 105–106.

4. **After lunch:** Using pages 71–76, guide participants in program evaluation (use PowerPoint to facilitate). Divide into groups and have teams develop a mock program and evaluation. Report out at end.

   Case Study (pages 9–19) [30 minutes], use Reflective Questions (page 19) as a guide.
   Summary and Evaluation (15 minutes)

* * * * * * * * * *

One-Day or Two-Day Workshop on any combination or all Seven Forms of Leadership: Instructional, Cultural, Ethical/Spiritual, Collaborative, School-Community, Operational, and Strategic

For one full-day workshop, you can cover any two forms of leadership by selecting agendas from the half-day format presented. For two full-day workshops, you can cover any four forms of leadership by selecting agendas from the half-day format presented.

For a two-day format, you can spend the first day on a general overview of all seven forms of leadership and the second day on a more in-depth discussion of one or two forms using any information in the half-day agenda presented.

Use PowerPoint at http://www.wagner.edu/faculty/jglanz/ppoint as a guide to the full-day workshop on all seven forms of leadership.

Workshop Evaluation Form

Content

How well did the workshop meet the goal and objectives?

How will you apply what you learned during this workshop in your daily professional life?

What professional support will you need to implement what you have learned from this workshop?

How well did the topics explored in this workshop meet a specific need in your school?

How relevant was this topic to your professional life?

Process

How well did the instructional techniques and activities facilitate your understanding of the topic?

How can you incorporate the activities learned today into your daily professional life?

Were a variety of learning experiences included in the workshop?

Was any particular activity memorable? What made it stand out?

Context

Were the facilities conducive to learning?

Were the accommodations adequate for the activities involved?

Overall

Overall, how successful would you consider this workshop? Please include a brief comment or explanation.

What was the most valuable thing you gained from this workshop experience?

SOURCE: Adapted from *Evaluating Professional Development* by Thomas R. Guskey, Corwin Press, Inc. 2000.

References

Alliance for Nonprofit Management. (2003–2004a). "The benefits of planning." Retrieved July 28, 2005, from http://www.allianceonline.org/FAQ/strategic_planning/what_do_i_need_to_know.faq

Biech, E. (Ed.). (2001). *The Pfeiffer book of successful team-building tools.* San Francisco: Jossey-Bass.

Blase, J., & Blase, J. (2004). *Handbook of instructional leadership: How successful principals promote teaching and learning.* Thousand Oaks, CA: Corwin Press.

Bolman, L. G., & Deal, T. E. (1997). *Reframing organizations: Artistry, choices, and leadership.* San Francisco: Jossey-Bass.

Bolton, R. (1986). *People skills.* New York: Touchstone.

Bruckner, M. (2004). The passion to lead. *Education Update, 46*(7), 2.

Chavkin, N. F. (2000). Family and community involvement policies: Teachers can lead the way. *The Clearing House, 73*(5), 287–293.

Cotton, K. (2003). *Principals and student achievement: What research says.* Alexandria, VA: Association for Supervision and Curriculum Development.

Davies, B., & Davies, B. J. (2005). Strategic leadership. In B. Davies (Ed.), *The essentials of school leadership* (pp. 10–30). London: Paul Chapman; Corwin Press.

Deal, T. E., & Peterson, K. D. (1999). *Shaping school culture: The heart of leadership.* San Francisco: Jossey-Bass.

Denham, C., & Michael, J. (1981). Teacher sense of efficacy: An important factor in school improvement. *Elementary School Journal, 86,* 173–184.

DeRoche, E. F. (1987). *An administrator's guide for evaluating programs and personnel: An effective schools approach* (2nd ed.). Boston: Allyn & Bacon.

Downey, C. J., Steffy, B. E., English, F. W., Frase, L. E., & Poston, W. K., Jr. (2004). *The three-minute walk-through: Changing school supervisory practice one teacher at a time.* Thousand Oaks, CA: Corwin Press.

Duffy, F. M. (2003). *Courage, passion, & vision: A guide to leading systemic school improvement.* Lanham, MD: Scarecrow Press.

Epstein, J. L., & Salinas, K. C. (2004). Partnering with families and communities. *Educational Leadership, 62*(3), 12–18.

Fashola, O. S. (2002). *Building effective after school programs.* Thousand Oaks, CA: Corwin Press.

Fiore, D. J. (2002). *School-community relations.* Larchmont, NY: Eye on Education.

Fullan, M., & Hargreaves, A. (1996). *What's worth fighting for in your school?* New York: Teachers College Press.

Gallegos Nava, R. (2001). *Holistic education: Pedagogy of universal love.* Brandon, VT: Foundation for Educational Renewal.

Glanz, J. (2002). *Finding your leadership style: A guide for educators.* Alexandria, VA: Association for Supervision and Curriculum Development.

Glatthorn, A. A. (2000). *Developing a quality curriculum.* Alexandria, VA: Association for Supervision and Curriculum Development.

Gretz, P. (2003). School and community partnerships: Cultivating friends. *Principal Leadership, 3*(5), 32–35.

Hare, W. (1993). *What makes a good teacher: Reflections on some characteristics central to the educational enterprise.* London: Althouse Press.

Haynes, N. M., & Emmons, C. L. (1997). *Comer school development program effects: A ten year review, 1986–1996.* New Haven, CT: Yale University Child Study Center.

Horsley, D. L., & Loucks-Horsley, S. (1998). CBAM brings order to the tornado of change. *Journal of Staff Development, 19*(4). Retrieved June 5, 2005, from http://www.nsdc.org/library/publications/jsd/horsley194.cfm

Hoyle, J. R. (2002). *Leadership and the force of love.* Thousand Oaks, CA: Corwin Press.

Kaser, J., Mundry, S., Loucks-Horsley, S., & Stiles, K. E. (2002). *Leading every day: 124 actions to effective leadership.* Thousand Oaks, CA: Corwin Press.

Keil, V. L. (2005). Communicating for results. *Principal Leadership, 5*(8), 28–31.

Kessler, R. (2000). *The soul of education: Helping students find connection, compassion, and character in school.* Alexandria, VA: Association for Supervision and Curriculum Development.

Komives, S. R., Lucas, N., & McMahon, T. R. (1998). *Exploring leadership.* San Francisco: Jossey-Bass.

Lawrence-Lightfoot, S. (2003). *The essential conversation: What parents and teachers can learn from each other.* New York: Random House.

Lucas, N., & Anello, E. (1995, November). *Ethics and leadership.* Paper presented at the Salzburg Leadership Seminar, Salzburg, Austria.

Lyddon, J. W. (1999). *Strategic planning in smaller nonprofit organizations: A practical guide for the process.* Kalamazoo: Nonprofit Leadership and Administration Faculty, Western Michigan University. Retrieved July 28, 2005, from http://www.wmich.edu/nonprofit/Guide/guide7.htm

Marazza, L. L. (2003). *The 5 essentials of organizational excellence: Maximizing schoolwide student achievement and performance.* Thousand Oaks, CA: Corwin Press.

Marzano, R. J. (2003). *What works in schools: Translating research into action.* Alexandria, VA: Association for Supervision and Curriculum Development.

Marzano, R. J., Pickering, D. J., & Pollock, J. E. (2001). *Classroom instruction that works: Research-based strategies for increasing student achievement.* Alexandria, VA: Association for Supervision and Curriculum Development.

Marzano, R. J., Waters, T., & McNully, B. A. (2005). *School leadership that works: From research to results.* Alexandria, VA: Association for Supervision and Curriculum Development.

Matthews, L. J., & Crow, G. M. (2003). *Being and becoming a principal: Role conceptions for contemporary assistant principals and principals.* Boston: Allyn & Bacon.

Mittenthal, R. (2002). *Ten keys to successful strategic planning* [briefing paper]. Philadelphia: Conservation Company.

Nash, L. L. (1990). *Good intentions aside.* Boston: Harvard Business School Press.

Null, G. (1996). *Who are you, really? Understanding your life's quality.* New York: Carroll & Graf.

Ogle, D. (1986) The K-W-L: A teaching model that develops active reading of expository text. *The Reading Teacher, 39,* 564–570.

Popham, W. J. (2001). *Classroom assessment: What teachers need to know.* Boston: Allyn & Bacon.

Ramsey, R. D. (2003). *School leadership from A to Z.* Thousand Oaks, CA: Corwin Press.

Rest, J. R. (1986). Moral development in young adults. In R. A. Mines & K. S. Kitchener (Eds.), *Adult cognitive development: Methods and models* (pp. 92–111). New York: Praeger.

Reynolds, M. (2002). Bringing your school closer to your community. *Principal Leadership (Middle Level Ed.), 3*(2), 81–82.

Robbins, P., & Alvy, H. B. (2003). *The principal's companion* (2nd ed.). Thousand Oaks, CA: Corwin Press.

Roberts, S., & Pruitt, E. (2003). *Schools as professional learning communities.* Thousand Oaks, CA: Corwin Press.

Rothstein, R. (2004). *Class and schools: Using social, economic, and educational reform to close the black-white achievement gap.* New York: Teachers College Press.

Sanders, M. G. (2001). The role of "community" in comprehensive school, family and community partnership programs. *The Elementary School Journal, 102*(1), 19–34.

Sanders, M. G., & Harvey, A. (2002). Beyond the school walls: A case study of principal leadership for school-community collaboration. *Teachers College Record, 104*(7), 1345–1368.

Sergiovanni, T. J. (1999). *Building community in schools.* San Francisco: Jossey-Bass.

Shaver, H. (2004). *Organize, communicate, empower: How principals can make time for leadership.* Thousand Oaks, CA: Corwin Press.

Simon, R. A., & Newman, J. F. (2004). *Making time to lead: How principals can stay on top of it all.* Thousand Oaks, CA: Corwin Press.

Squires, D. A., Huitt, W. G., & Segars, J. K. (1984). *Effective schools and classrooms: A research-based perspective.* Alexandria, VA: Association for Supervision and Curriculum Development.

Starratt, R. J. (1996). *Transforming educational administration: Meaning, community, and excellence.* New York: McGraw-Hill.

Stronge, J. H. (2002). *Qualities of effective teaching.* Alexandria, VA: Association for Supervision and Curriculum Development.

Sullivan, S., & Glanz, J. (2006). *Building effective learning communities: Strategies for leadership, learning, & collaboration.* Thousand Oaks, CA: Corwin Press.

Sullivan, S., & Glanz, J. (2005). *Supervision that improves teaching: Strategies and techniques* (2nd ed.). Thousand Oaks, CA: Corwin Press.

Thompson, S. (2004). Leading from the eye of the storm. *Educational Leadership, 61*(7), 60–63.

Tyler, R. W. (1949). *Basic principles of curriculum and instruction.* Chicago: University of Chicago Press.

Ubben, G. C., Hughes, L. W., & Norris, C. J. (2004). *The principal: Creative leadership for excellence in schools* (5th ed.). Boston: Allyn & Bacon.

Waters, J. T., Marzano, R. J., & McNulty, B. (2004). Leadership that sparks learning. *Educational Leadership, 61*(7), 48–51.

Whitaker, K. S. (1995). Principal burnout: Implications for professional development. *Journal of Personnel Evaluation in Education, 9,* 287–296.

Whitaker, T., & Fiore, D. (2001). *Dealing with difficult parents (and with parents in difficult situations).* New York: Eye on Education.

Wiles, J., & Bondi, J. (1998). *Curriculum development: A guide to practice.* Upper Saddle River, NJ: Prentice Hall.

Young, P. G. (2004). *You have to go to school—You're the principal: 101 tips to make it better for your students, your staff, and yourself.* Thousand Oaks, CA: Corwin Press.

Zubay, B., & Soltis, J. (2005). *Creating the ethical school: A book of case studies.* New York: Teachers College Press.

**CORWIN
PRESS**

The Corwin Press logo—a raven striding across an open book—represents the union of courage and learning. Corwin Press is committed to improving education for all learners by publishing books and other professional development resources for those serving the field of PreK–12 education. By providing practical, hands-on materials, Corwin Press continues to carry out the promise of its motto: **"Helping Educators Do Their Work Better."**

Printed in the United States
By Bookmasters